Claas Friedrich Germelmann (ed.)

# Innovative Teaching in European Legal Education

International Conference within the Framework of the
2019 ELPIS Network Meeting

HART
PUBLISHING

**Nomos**

**The Deutsche Nationalbibliothek** lists this publication in the Deutsche Nationalbibliografie; detailed bibliographic data are available on the Internet at http://dnb.d-nb.de

ISBN:     HB (Nomos)          978-3-8487-7950-5
          ePDF (Nomos)        978-3-7489-2333-6


**British Library Cataloguing-in-Publication Data**
A catalogue record for this book is available from the British Library.

ISBN:     HB (Hart)           9781509954421


**Library of Congress Cataloging-in-Publication Data**
Germelmann, Claas Friedrich
Innovative Teaching in European Legal Education
International Conference within the Framework of the
2019 ELPIS Network Meeting
Claas Friedrich Germelmann (ed.)
176 pp.
Includes bibliographic references and index.

ISBN     9781509954421       (hardcover Hart)

Onlineversion
Nomos eLibrary

1st Edition 2021
© Nomos Verlagsgesellschaft, Baden-Baden, Germany 2021. Overall responsibility for manufacturing (printing and production) lies with Nomos Verlagsgesellschaft mbH & Co. KG.

# Preface

Modernising legal education is a daunting task. Finding a common ground for legal education in Europe, let alone in an international perspective, is even more difficult. Nevertheless, the challenges of the modern world, the complexity and interconnectivity that globalisation is bringing about for the law and the legal professions, and the technological progress in the field of digitalisation require changes in the traditional patterns of domestic legal education. University education as a whole is facing challenges, but it is also experiencing new opportunities as not only the current health crisis and the forced change to a variety of online tools replacing and complementing traditional lectures and classroom work have shown. More generally, the requirements of legal professions and the needs of law students are changing, and legal education has to address these changes.

Hence, in recent years, modernising legal education has become an endeavour of growing interest in the academic world. Both the international point of view and the digitalisation issue are core topics in the discourse. It was therefore obvious to bring the question of innovative teaching in law up within the framework of the ELPIS network, which has been assembling a significant (and growing) number of scholars from European and non-European law faculties since its founding by professor *Hilmar Fenge* of Hanover university in the 1980s. Throughout its history, the network's focus has always been on an active exchange on questions of legal education. The collective volume takes up this topic and assembles several essays of scholars of the ELPIS network on different topics of modern legal education. The contributions are based on the talks and discussions as well as on the ideas developed at the annual conference of 2019. It took place in Hanover in December, at a time when no one would have thought that the global health crisis that broke loose only a few weeks after would have a catalytic effect on the changes and challenges in legal education throughout the world.

The contributions take different points of view on the topic of modern legal education, combining comparative, European and global perspectives. They focus on the value of international exchange, on questions of law curricula and on employability requirements in a globalised world, on students' needs and on modern teaching methods, and especially on various instruments of digitalised learning, teaching and publishing. While by no means intending to deliver a final concept for modern legal education, the book wishes to show the diversity of the fields as well as the variety of challenges that have to be addressed. It will hopefully be offering some guidance in this area and contribute to the continuing debate which not only the health crisis has proven to be an important and timely one.

I would like to thank our publishers, NOMOS and Hart Publishing, and in particular professor *Johannes Rux*, for the support and assistance in the publishing process. I furthermore wish to thank Dr *Dimitrios Parashu* for his help in organising the conference as well as for his assistance with the work for this volume. Finally, I would like to express my gratitude to all the participants of the Hanover conference where many of the ideas have been discussed and tested. The continuing exchange within the network has proven to be particularly fruitful in times when online teaching has become the new normal.

Hanover, January 2021                                                 *Claas Friedrich Germelmann*

# Table of Contents

# Challenges and Approaches to Modern Legal Education in a European Perspective

*Claas Friedrich Germelmann* *

## A. Legal methodology and legal education: A relationship determined by tradition and stability?

The fact that the world has been becoming more and more interconnected and complex during the last decades and the observation that this development has taken up an immense speed by way of globalisation and technical progress notably in the field of digitalisation is a mere commonplace. That does not mean, however, that the challenges and consequences of these developments have already been fully ascertained with a view to the different fields of university education. It is probably not even possible to realise and to describe in a clear-cut pattern and with a predictable timeframe all the new opportunities and new conflicts that these changes are about to create in the years lying immediately ahead and in the medium-term future. Even if it were conceivable to formulate a "mission of the university" today as *José Ortega y Gasset* described it in 1930[1], or to develop an "idea of the university" as *Karl Jaspers* put it after the two major catastrophes of the 20th century[2], it would have to remain open to significant changes because of these new challenges.

* Prof. Dr. Claas Friedrich Germelmann, LL.M. (Cantab.), Gottfried Wilhelm Leibniz University of Hanover (Chair for Public Law and European Law).

1 Ortega y Gasset, José, *Schuld und Schuldigkeit der Universität*, Munich, Verlag R. Oldenbourg, 1952 (original Spanish version: *La misión de la universidad*, Madrid, 1930).
2 Jaspers, Karl, *Die Idee der Universität*, Berlin and Heidelberg, Springer-Verlag, 1946. A previous edition dates back to 1923. Last edition: Jaspers, Karl and Rossmann, Kurt, *Die Idee der Universität für die gegenwärtige Situation*, Berlin and Heidelberg, Springer-Verlag, 1961.

## I. The role of tradition in legal education

These changes will be noticeable in legal education too, although this area of university studies tends to be a particularly traditional field[3]. Even taking into account the challenges, which the universities and their study programmes had to meet during the last decades, as *e.g.* in the form of the realignments by the Bologna process in Europe[4], and despite the growing numbers of students, an increasingly diverse policy framework and severe financial cuttings, legal education remains, in its core, a rather stable field. That follows mainly from its being dependent on texts like legal acts, court decisions and treaties which themselves stem from longstanding traditions of law making and administering justice. In some jurisdictions, notably in those that are based on the common law system, tradition and traditional approaches necessarily play a highly important role, which is connected with a long-standing approach of interpreting and "learning the law"[5]. The civil law jurisdictions do not represent a strong contrast to that by definition. Tradition and stability are undisputed values here as well. In German legal methodology *e.g.*, the approach and the methods that *Friedrich Carl von Savigny* established in the middle of the 19th century[6], still represent the core standards of legal interpretation[7]. Similarly, in international law, the interpretation and application of legal rules rest, for a major part, upon longstanding international custom and have not changed significantly throughout the last century[8].

Law *in its nature* therefore tends to be a rather immobile subject irrespective of how lively and modern some areas might appear. The speed in

---

3 Borman, Deborah L. and Haras, Catherine, *Something Borrowed: Interdisciplinary Strategies for Legal Education*, (2019) 68 Journal of Legal Education 357, 358: "Law, known for its reticence if not conservatism with regard to innovating classroom instruction […]".

4 See, for an outline of the process, the official European Higher Education Area website (http://www.ehea.info/index.php; 2.1.2021).

5 *Cf.* the title of the classic book of Glanville Williams, *Learning the Law*, 17th edition by A.T.H. Smith, London, Sweet & Maxwell, 2020.

6 Von Savigny, Friedrich Carl, *System des heutigen römischen Rechts*, Vol. 1, § 33, pp. 212-6, Berlin, Veit und Comp., 1840.

7 See, e.g., Larenz, Karl and Canaris, Claus-Wilhelm, Methodenlehre der Rechtswissenschaft, 3rd edition, Berlin and Heidelberg, Springer-Verlag, 1995, Ch. 4.

8 Cf. the articles 31 to 33 of the Vienna Convention on the Law of Treaties of 1969, which reflect international customary law. See, in more detail and with further references, Shaw, Malcolm N., *International Law*, 8th edition, Cambridge, Cambridge University Press, 2017, pp. 706-11.

which modern administrative law concerning trade, industry and regulation is developing leaves legal scholars and practitioners with but little time in order to create convincing general dogmatic structures and foreseeable patterns. One particularly striking example is the sector of environmental law[9], but the same applies to other comparable modern fields as *e.g.* energy law[10], where the complex multi-level structure is encompassing international law as well as domestic and (potentially) European law and is, on top of that, constantly expanding.

That does not mean, however, that these modern developments and the pace of change in these legal areas would necessarily have led to significant changes in legal teaching. On the contrary, the basic approach in these subjects is mostly still more or less similar to legal teaching in traditional areas of law. That follows, at least in part, from the fact that the legislator as well as the courts quite rightly treat those fields like "normal" areas of law and therefore subject them to the same patterns of interpretation and application as law in general. From a constitutional point of view, it would not be possible to distinguish between different sets of legal norms that are formally on the same footing, address in a similar way questions that have to be settled in a conclusive manner and require to be followed in the same way. A different approach might be conceivable only in the area of non-binding standards and soft law[11], which, at least in Germany, however, still do not play a significant role in legal education[12]. When legal practise does not distinguish between different of areas of law, it requires a similar treatment of them also in the field of legal education.

---

9 For an overview of the legal rules after the Paris Agreement of 2015, see Bodansky, Daniel, *The Paris Climate Change Agreement: A New Hope?*, 110 (2016) AJIL 288; Rajamani, Lavanya, *Ambition and Differentiation in the 2015 Paris Agreement: Interpretive Possibilities and Underlying Politics*, 65 (2016) ICLQ 493; Bodansky, Daniel and Rajamani, Lavanya, *The Issues that Never Die*, [2018] CCLR 184; van Asselt, Harro, Kulovesi, Kati, and Mehling, Michael, *Negotiating the Paris Rulebook*, [2018] CCLR 173. Furthermore, see the *Paris Agreement Work Programme (PAWP)* included in the decision 1/CP.21 *Adoption of the Paris Agreement*, FCCC/CP/2015/10/Add.1.

10 See, for an overview, Roggenkamp, Martha, Redgwell, Catherine, Rønne, Anita, and del Guayo, Iñigo (eds.), *Energy Law in Europe. National, EU and International Regulation*, 3rd edition, Oxford, Oxford University Press, 2016.

11 See, for an overview from the European perspective, Senden, Linda, *Soft Law in European Community Law*, Oxford and Portland (Oregon), Hart Publishing, 2004; Knauff, Matthias, *Der Regelungsverbund: Recht und Soft Law im Mehrebenensystem*, Tübingen, Mohr Siebeck, 2010.

12 For a critical recent assessment, Knauff, Matthias, *Soft Law vor Gericht*, jM 2018, p. 71.

## II. European Union law as an example of a modern legal order

A challenge that could have prompted a fundamentally different approach in legal education was the introduction of the law of the European Communities, which is, today, the law of the European Union. While the choice of the example might seem astonishing at first, European Union law can still be considered a rather modern form of law. It not only combines different approaches of rulemaking for a variety of substantially diverse legal orders in sometimes rather controversial areas, but it is also significantly influencing the law and policy of the Member States and is shaping their response to actual legal problems. Despite its age and success, it therefore can still serve as an example for some basic challenges, which modern legal orders and modern legal education have to face. In this respect, it is obviously less about the substantive law contents of European Union law. Rather, the main emphasis is on the general competences and skills that it is requiring from a modern lawyer. In other legal orders outside the European Union, the globalisation of the law will create similar challenges to law students and practising lawyers[13].

### 1. The specific features of European Union law in legal education

According to the well-known phrase of the European Court of Justice, European Union law is a "new legal order"[14]. Hence, it has its own structures and commands specific features that distinguish it from both the legal orders of the Member States and from public international law. Nevertheless, by its nature, it remains law and thus has to be treated as such not only by its addressees, *i.e.* especially the branches of government in the Member States, but also by legal education. The way in which law curricu-

---

13 See, for the US, the UK and China, respectively, Flood, John, *Global Challenges to Legal Education*, in: Gane, Christopher and Huang, Robin Hui (eds.), *Legal Education in the Global Context*, London and New York, Routledge, 2016, p. 31; Xiaohong, Liu, *Cultivating High-Quality Internationalized Legal Talents under Legal Globalization*, in: Gane, Christopher and Huang, Robin Hui (eds.), *Legal Education in the Global Context*, London and New York, Routledge, 2016, p. 87.

14 ECJ, 5 February 1963, Case 26/62 (*van Gend & Loos*), [1963] ECR 12; 15 July 1964, Case 6/64 (*Costa* v. *ENEL*), [1964] ECR 593; 18 December 2014, Opinion 2/13 (*Accession of the European Union to the ECHR*), para. 157; 10 December 2018, Case 621/18 (*Wightman*), para. 44.

la in the Member States have incorporated it rightly stresses its being a part of the family of legal rules and embraces its particularities in the existing patterns of legal education. The same applies to those extra-European countries in which European Union law is being taught as an example of a special legal order of international law. In German legal education, however, the appearance of EU law did not give rise to a fundamental shift neither in methodological teaching nor with regard to the basic didactic instruments. Quite to the contrary, European Community law (as it then was) mostly used to be treated from a perspective either of traditional public international law or (regarding the institutional parts) in the tradition of German constitutional law. Given the specific dogmatic tradition of European law, however, neither seems to have been inappropriate. Modern legal education has to take into account the holistic approach that the extensive competences of the Union permeating the entire legal orders of the Member States undisputedly require[15].

Its special characteristics and its specific situation in legal education, however, are evident even if one ignores, for that matter, the details of how European Union law has managed to impose itself on the legal orders of the Member States. Its unique choices relating to the institutional structure of the Union, the repartition of competences and its relationship to the constitutional orders of the Member States[16] are just parts of the substantive law contents of European legal teaching. The specific methodological features of European Union law that are particularly relevant for a competence-based legal teaching tend to distinguish themselves from some traditional points of view in domestic law.

## 2. Multilingualism

Among the most obvious characteristics of European law are the challenges connected with multilingualism[17]. Even if the institutions of the

---

15  One of the first victims is the strict public-private law divide that the German legal tradition still holds dear.

16  See, *e.g.*, Hartley, Trevor C., *The Foundations of European Union Law*, 8th edition, Oxford, Oxford University Press, 2014, Ch. 7 and 8.

17  See, for more details, Pingel, Isabelle (ed.), *Le multilinguisme dans l'Union européenne*, Paris, Pedone, 2015; Juaristi, Patxi, Reagan, Timothy and Tonkin, Humphrey, *Language diversity in the European Union. An overview*, in: Arzoz, Xabier (ed.), *Respecting Linguistic Diversity in the European Union*, Amsterdam, John Benjamins Publishing Company, 2008, pp. 47-72.

European Union cannot always fully maintain an equal treatment of the official languages in their day-to-day work, article 55, para. 1, TEU sets a clear statement as to the requirements concerning legal acts[18]. The regime relating to the use of languages in the European Court of Justice is a similar example[19]. According to article 41, para. 4, CFR and article 24, para. 4, TFEU, the equality of languages even is a fundamental right. However, the equality of the Member States' languages is not a general principle of law, which claims to be absolute. Quite in contrast, the European Court of Justice has accepted on several occasions that, under certain circumstances, restrictions may apply if they are necessary in order to maintain the proper functioning of the EU institutions and if they prove proportionate with a view to the interests of the parties involved[20].

## 3. Comparative law

Apart from that, European Union law is not only decisively influenced by multilingualism, it is also marked by the impact of the different legal orders and the diversity of the legal cultures of the Member States. That necessitates, in some fields, a comparative legal approach in the strict sense of the word[21]. The prime example has been the traditional shaping and interpretation of European fundamental rights prior to the enactment of the Charter of Fundamental Rights of the Union. Article 6, para. 3, TEU still maintains this approach as an additional strand of protection besides the Charter[22]. The same applies to other areas in the case law of the European

---

18  See, for the corresponding rule in general international law, article 33 of the Vienna Convention on the Law of Treaties of 1969.
19  See articles 36-42 of the Rules of Procedure of the Court of Justice, [2012] OJ L 265, p. 1.
20  ECJ, 9 September 2003, Case C-361/01 P (*Kik* v. *OHMI*), [2003] ECR I-8283, para. 92; 12 May 2011, Case C-410/09 (*Polska Telefonia Cyfrowa*), [2011] ECR I-3853, para. 38; 5 May 2015, Case C-147/13 (*Spain* v. *Council*), paras. 31-48.
21  Concerning the comparative law method, *cf.*, *e.g.*, Kischel, Uwe, *Rechtsvergleichung*, Munich, Verlag C.H. Beck, 2015, Ch. 3.
22  See General Court, 6 February 2014, Case T-27/10 (*AC-Treuhand AG* v. *Commission*), para. 170. For that reason, comparative law elements can still influence indirectly the interpretation of the Charter of Fundamental Rights, which, according to article 6, para. 1, TEU is on an equal footing. The same applies to the influence of the European Convention of Human Rights owing to article 52, para. 3, CFR; see ECJ, 26 February 2013, Case C-617/10 (*Åkerberg Fransson*), para. 44; 16 July 2020, Case C-311/18 (*Schrems no. 2*), para. 98.

Court of Justice where it is developing legal concepts in accordance with the traditional legal orders of the Member States[23]. An example is the liability for breaches of European Union law committed by the Union[24] and by the Member States[25].

On top of that, a comparative technique in a broader sense can be relevant in the development of legal texts in European secondary legislation. This might not be indispensable for technical issues and in fields where the European legislator sets out to create an entirely new branch of regulatory rules. Compromise solutions, however, that try to insert new European law impulses into more established areas of domestic law might increase their acceptance if they are at least informed by or leave room to the legal traditions of the Member States[26]. This example of a broader comparative perspective, which pays attention to national peculiarities and traditional legal cultures, becomes most important when dealing with fundamental constitutional principles or, for the lack of a more precise description, constitutional identities of the Member States[27]. The primary law of the Union supports this approach with a view to article 4, para. 2, TEU and article 22 CFR.

---

23  For the principle of proportionality, see ECJ, 17 December 1970, Case 11/70 (*Internationale Handelsgesellschaft*), [1970] ECR 1125. For the comparative law influence, especially of German law, *cf.*, in more detail, Craig, Paul, *EU Administrative Law*, 3<sup>rd</sup> edition, Oxford, Oxford University Press, 2018, Ch. 19 and 20.
24  Article 340, paras. 2, 3, TFEU makes a direct reference to the legal orders of the Member States in terms of state liability. Concerning the question of liability for lawful acts, see ECJ, 9 September 2008, Cases C-120/06 P and C-121/06 P (*Fabbrica italiana accumulatori motocarri Montecchio – FIAMM*), [2008] ECR I-6513, paras. 170-9.
25  See ECJ, 5 March 1996, Cases C-46/93 and C-48/93 (*Brasserie du Pêcheur and Factortame*), [1996] ECR I-1029, paras. 28-32.
26  See, by way of example, concerning the transposition of the Distance Selling Directive into German law, Flume, Werner, *Vom Beruf unserer Zeit für Gesetzgebung – Die Änderungen des BGB durch das Fernabsatzgesetz*, ZIP 2000, 1427.
27  *Cf.*, by way of example, the recent controversies between the European Court of Justice and, respectively, the Italian and German constitutional courts: Corte costituzionale, 23 November 2016, ordinanza 24/2017, ECLI:IT:COST:2017:24; 10 April 2018, sentenza 115/2018, ECLI:IT:COST:2018:115 (*"Taricco"* case); Bundesverfassungsgericht, 18 July 2017, 2 BvR 859/15 *et al.*, BVerfGE 146, 216; 5 May 2020, 2 BvR 859/15 *et al.*, BVerfGE 154, 17 (*"PSPP"* case).

## 4. Case law and methods of interpretation

The case law of the European Court of Justice is another, particularly rich source for identifying the challenges of modern legal methodology. It starts with the increasing importance of case law in general, which is affecting even the European civil law jurisdictions. Further elements are the abovementioned challenges as to multilingualism and comparative law, which particularly relate to the Court's case law. It goes on with the methods of interpretation, which the European Court of Justice is using and which transcend the traditionally predominant limits of textual interpretation in the decisions of international courts and tribunals[28]. Owing to its style of drafting its decisions, the Court still leaves significant room for debates in the legal doctrine. Finally, it has created several interpretative rules that, like the principle of effectiveness or *effet utile*, have gained a cross cutting relevance as some of the most notable teleological specialities of European Union law[29].

## B. Challenges to modern legal education

The short, necessarily fragmentary and cursory description of the challenges with which European Union law is confronting traditional legal methods and ways of legal teaching highlights some of the substantive legal innovations that cannot only be found in this particular area of law,

---

28  See, for more detail of the methods of interpretation used by the European Court of Justice, Lenaerts, Koen and Gutierrez-Fons, José A., *To Say What the Law of the EU Is: Methods of Interpretation and the European Court of Justice*, (2014) 20 Colum-JEurL 3; Conway, Gerard, *The Limits of Legal Reasoning and the European Court of Justice*, Cambridge, Cambridge University Press, 2012, Ch. 3.

29  *Cf.*, *e.g.*, ECJ, 4 December, Case 41/74 (*van Duyn*), [1974] ECR 1337, para. 12; 9 March 1978, Case 106/77 (*Simmenthal*), [1978] ECR 629), para. 20; 20 March 1997, Case C-24/95 (*Alcan II*) [1997] ECR I-1591, para. 37; for a more detailed analysis, Tomasic, Lovro, *Effet utile: Die Relativität teleologischer Argumente im Unionsrechts*, Munich, Verlag C.H. Beck, 2013. The principle of effectiveness plays a significant role in public international law as well, as the ICJ pointed out correctly in its *Fisheries Jurisdiction (Spain v. Canada)* case, ICJ Reports, 1999, p. 432, 455. However, the European *effet utile* goes even further than that given the much higher degree of integration in the European Union. See, on this matter, Bobek, Michal, *The Court of Justice of the European Union*, in: Arnull, Anthony and Chalmers, Damian (eds.), *The Oxford Handbook of European Union Law*, Oxford, Oxford University Press, 2015, pp. 153, 173-5.

but which appear on a broader international scene. Domestic legal orders as well as transnational law making and adjudication have to consider them and to offer solutions. So has modern legal education. Examining the European legal challenges can possibly help to find a path to understanding and further developing modern international and European legal education.

### I. *Multilingualism and different legal cultures*

That applies, first, to the growing importance of multilingualism and of the awareness for different legal cultures. Under the current system, domestic law is just one element in the large jigsaw of the legal orders in the international community. It is heavily influenced by foreign legal decisions be it from the international or from the supranational legal sphere. Understanding the structure of these connections and, ideally, of some basic influential concepts helps a lot when interpreting domestic law and, obviously, when shaping domestic choices that will enter into the international competition of legal instruments and concepts[30]. The challenge for modern legal education is therefore to enable future lawyers to be able to follow and to understand international influences on domestic law. The more international the education becomes the more influential its ideas can possibly get since it will be able to encompass the legal positions of other legal cultures and understand their interrelationship. That, however, requires sound competences in the field of languages as well as some comparative skills.

### II. *Increased factual complexity*

The second challenge is the increasing factual complexity that requires a basic understanding for the relevant situations governed by the legal framework. Hence, not only traditional, but also new methods of regulation will have to be included in modern legal teaching. In several instances, the experiences not only of European Union law, but also of international law show that traditional legal instruments often reach their lim-

---

30 For the political controversies in the field of climate change law, see, *e.g.*, Bodansky, Daniel and Rajamani, Lavanya, *The Issues that Never Die*, [2018] CCLR 184.

its and have to be supplemented with alternative means of regulation and dispute settlement. The examples for this are manifold; among the most prominent is the international, European and domestic combat against climate change with the Paris Agreement[31] and the EU governance system[32], which, notably, do not exclusively contain legally binding rules, but also alternative approaches of soft law[33]. In a similar way, modern administrative or economic laws show the tendency to regulate by way of influencing rather than by way of ordering and compelling. The challenge for modern legal education consists in explaining and classifying these alternative ways of regulation and in highlighting their potential, but also their dangers with a view to the repartition of competences, fundamental rights and basic legal principles.

## III. Systematic approaches and the role of case law

A third challenge can be seen in the increasing role of case law originating from different levels in the international sphere, like it is especially, but not exclusively the case in the area of human rights, concerning the decisions of the European Court of Justice, the European Court of Human Rights and domestic jurisdictions. International arbitration plays an additional important role, particularly in the field of economic law. Case law is shaping the international and supranational legal orders and has a major impact on domestic law making and the application of legal rules. In order to know the law, it is indispensable to know an ever more complex and rich case law that sometimes even the legislator uses as a model for policy decisions. Naturally, this development is by no means a new and unprecedented one. Quite on the contrary, the decision of courts and tribunals have always shaped the law even in civil law jurisdictions. It is, however,

---

31  Decision 1/CP.21 *Adoption of the Paris Agreement*, FCCC/CP/2015/10/Add.1.
32  Regulation (EU) 2018/1999 of the European Parliament and of the Council of 11 December 2018 on the Governance of the Energy Union and Climate Action, [2018] OJ L 328, p. 1.
33  See, more generally, on these issues from an international law perspective, Brunnée, Jutta, *COPing with Consent: Law-Making Under Multilateral Environmental Agreements*, 15 (2002) LeidenJIntL 1; Germelmann, Claas Friedrich, *Moderne Rechtssetzungsformen im Umweltvölkerrecht – Entwicklung und Perspektiven sekundärrechtlicher Regelungsmechanismen*, 52 (2014) AVR 325. See also Micklitz, Hans-Wolfgang, *The Bifurcation of Legal Education – National vs Transnational*, in: Gane, Christopher and Huang, Robin Hui (eds.), *Legal Education in the Global Context*, London and New York, Routledge, 2016, p. 43, 56.

the complexity and the diversity that are constantly growing and that are creating more and more fields of sometimes-intricate specialisation. The knowledge of case law is indispensable in legal education because of the high influence of the judiciary on both the lawmakers and those who apply the law like public administrations. The growing degree of special expertise and the increasing role of case law in an environment where legislators often openly leave complex legal questions for the courts to decide, encounter the need to reduce complexity in legal education in order to prevent the time of studies from wearing on indefinitely. It therefore seems necessary to keep a focus on the general and basic skills and competences from which a specialised knowledge can develop. This, however, requires a sound methodology in dealing with case law, which, obviously, is far more refined in common law traditions than in civil law systems or, for that matter, in European Union law.

## IV. Methods of teaching

Modern legal education thus faces a vast number of challenges as far as substantive and methodological questions of law and the law curricula are concerned[34]. Practical methods of teaching, in fact, are another highly important field when talking about modernising the common standards of legal studies.

It is true that the digitalisation has brought several new opportunities many of which have become even more apparent during the pandemic of the years of 2020 and 2021. While digitalisation thus presents enormous chances in modern legal education not only concerning the accessibility of sources[35], but also relating to new opportunities in teaching, as several of the articles in this volume will show[36], it comes along with problems that

---

34 See, for an overview, Heringa, Aalt Willem, *Legal Education: Reflections and Recommendations*, Cambridge, Antwerp and Portland, Intersentia 2013, especially Ch. 7-12.

35 Concerning this matter, *cf.* the contributions focusing on course materials in: Rubin, Edward (ed.), *Legal Education in the Digital Age*, Cambridge, Cambridge University Press, 2012.

36 See the contributions in this volume by Pereira da Silva, Vasco, *"My Fair Lady": Introductive Lecture*, p. 41; Balaguer Callejón, Francisco, *Modern Teaching Methods in European Legal Education*, p. 53; Jovanov, Kire, *'Jigsaw Classroom' and Law Teaching*, p. 87; Künnecke, Arndt, *The Flipped Classroom Approach in Legal Education*, p. 97; Hugg, Patrick R., *Perspectives from the United States: Pioneering in Legal Education as Innovation Advances*, p. 129; Guerra da Fonseca, Rui, *Distance Learn-*

cannot all be discarded easily. A major issue that cannot be addressed in detail here are questions of data protection that the European legislation tends to deal with in a rather restrictive way[37] and which thus may hinder the opportunities of a free and uncomplicated academic exchange. New technologies, moreover, tend to alter the way in which university researchers as well as students are able to express and to live their academic freedoms. This can be both challenging and a key to new opportunities[38]. From an organisational point of view, common distance learning of collaborative law classes in different countries all over the world, however, can become one of the major achievements of digitalisation in legal education[39].

Another practical problem that will have to be solved in the near future are online assessments and the question of how to control the compliance with examination regulations and the rules of good scientific practise in case of online exams. Moreover, some contents and competences in legal education seem to be less suitable for online distance teaching. University studies in general, and among them legal studies in particular, necessarily involve an active exchange of arguments. The university has to be a forum for an unfettered discourse that develops and thoroughly tests scientific results and views. That is not only due to its "mission" in a democratic society, but follows also from its tasks to prepare the students for their future professional occupations. In that context, it is clear that an effective settlement of disputes needs the entire spectrum of verbal and non-verbal reactions, which an online exchange alone cannot provide. The traditional ways of university teaching therefore must never disappear entirely since they are the only way to train lawyers to command the full extent of skills they are in need of in order to fulfil their future tasks in an efficient and legitimate way.

---

*ing and Video-Based Academic Contributions: Steps Towards "A World Made New"?*, p. 147; Rigó, Balázs, *From the Student Circle of Playing Legal Cases through the Mentorprogramme to Social Responsibility*, p. 157.

37 *Cf.* regulation (EU) 2016/679 of the European Parliament and of the Council of 27 April 2016 on the protection of natural persons with regard to the processing of personal data and on the free movement of such data, [2016] OJ L 119, p. 1, and especially the conditions for a voluntary consent to data processing according to article 7 of the regulation.

38 See Balaguer Callejón, Francisco, *Modern Teaching Methods in European Legal Education*, in this volume, p. 53.

39 See Hugg, Patrick R., *Perspectives from the United States: Pioneering in Legal Education as Innovation Advances*, in this volume, p. 129.

## C. Potential answers

It follows from the above that modern legal education is confronted with growing factual and legal complexities, a higher degree of international and supranational interaction and increased opportunities of teaching methods in a more and more digitalised world. As far as this contribution is concerned, there are no definitive answers to the challenges that have been described above. It only wishes to submit some suggestions that could potentially address them and contribute to bringing legal teaching more in line with what modern law is requiring.

### I. Adding new elements: Changing methods or piling up content?

In any event, two points must not be disregarded in the entire discussion about improving and modernising legal education.

First, as far as legal methodology is concerned, the traditional approaches have proven to be not only resilient, but also effective and capable of solving legal problems in a differentiated and overall just and equitable manner. From the point of view of a European lawyer, there is no need for any radical change in this field. On the contrary, the suitability of the current methodology to rationalise debates and disputes cannot be underestimated. The suggestions therefore can only consist in additional elements to the positive and well-proven portfolio of current legal education.

That leads to the second caveat. In fact, legal teaching is constantly facing the problem of an information overload. The more complex the legal structures and their underlying factual situations are the more substantive law contents law classes have to convey. It is not possible, however, to simply amend the curricula by piling up information and to extend the time for studies[40]. Therefore, the suggestions always have to respect the necessity of limiting to a reasonable extent the substance law students will have to command and thus of prioritising structure and methodology in contrast to an overly specialised expertise. There is indeed a difference between the sophisticated dogmatic methodology of a national legal system, which is worth preserving, and a complexity stemming from an ever-increasing spe-

---

40  For a more detailed analysis regarding the challenges of law curricula with a view to comparative law and with a comparative approach, Schwartze, Andreas, *A more European Legal Education – Lessons to be Learned*, in this volume, p. 67, with further references.

cialisation in case law and regulation. It is necessary that the students are up to date as far as major developments in the case law of the courts are concerned. Apart from that, a thorough understanding of general concepts and methods seems superior to any specialised knowledge and, furthermore, is serving creative and critical reasoning in a far better way. This premise indicates the path to take when dealing with modern features like soft law and alternative methods of regulation. It is rather the structural peculiarities, the new problems and the general principles governing these fields that are relevant for legal education. The teaching therefore should primarily focus on them and highlight some examples, which can be conveyed by way of case studies. University legal education needs to enable the students to critically assess the general lines of law making and of legal practise and has to show them how to draw connecting lines. Law is not an applied science and therefore, even with the use of modern facilities like *e.g.* digitalised contents, legal education should not be tempted into treating it as such.

## II. Increasing interdisciplinary and comparative competences

As the factual situations, which legal rules have to address and to regulate, are becoming more and more complex, it follows directly that the competences of law students in the relevant fields need to be strengthened and improved[41]. At the same time, legal education has to respect the unique character of law[42] as a core constitutional concept that engages democratic legitimation. The overall complexity, however, makes it impossible to cov-

---

41 See, on this topic, Meng-Papantoni, Maria, *The Teaching of Legal Practice in Europe: An Outlook*, in this volume, p. 119; Balsam, Jodi S., *Teaming Up to learn in the Doctrinal Classroom*, (2019) 68 Journal of Legal Education 261, 273. From the point of view of legal practise, see the „overall skill-set" that is being proposed by Smith, Alexander and Spencer, Nigel, *Do Lawyers Need to Learn to Code? A Practitioner Perspective on the 'Polytechnic' Future of Legal Education*, in: Devir, Catrina (ed.), Modernising Legal Education, Cambridge, Cambridge University Press, 2020, pp. 18, 31-2.

42 An undistinguished "interdisciplinary", "contextual" approach to the law itself can therefore at best be complimentary and cannot alter the mission of law and hence the specific requirements of legal education. The suggestions made by Galloway, Kate, *Getting Back to Our Roots: Global Law Schools in Local Context*, in: Gane, Christopher and Huang, Robin Hui (eds.), *Legal Education in the Global Context*, London and New York, Routledge, 2016, pp. 17, 23-30, thus have to be considered with some caution.

er even in a superficial way every single field in science and humanities that might at some point become directly or indirectly relevant for legal education. The times of scholars specialising in entirely different disciplines at the same time have long since passed, and such a model would not even be in the slightest way helpful for a practising lawyer whose expertise is needed in a rather narrowly limited field of law like domestic tax law or domestic criminal law. Therefore, interdisciplinary competence can reasonably be obtained only in a small number of rather specific fields if it is meant to further the quality of administering justice or representing clients. A notable, but rather specific example are agents in the field of industrial property.

Generally, it seems more important that lawyers learn to understand the broad patterns of argumentation in academic fields like natural or political sciences, economics or engineering and are open to their levels of discussion. Since it would be far too time consuming to implement entire study programmes of these disciplines into legal studies, the majority of the law faculties in Germany require the students to enrol for some form of detached lectures mostly relating to economics during the basic part of their studies. It seems doubtful, however, if those lectures, which are often designed for law students only, really increase the capability of an interdisciplinary exchange. For those purposes, it might be more efficient to implement some interdisciplinary elements in lectures or seminars on a more advanced level[43] when students will be fitter to interconnect specific legal questions, *e.g.* from the field of environmental law, with the correlating problems in other disciplines like environmental planning, meteorology, engineering or economics. Instead of the more traditional approach of offering lectures in different disciplines specifically for law students, it might be advisable rather to combine lectures and interdisciplinary seminars with students from a variety of disciplines since the core competence lies in the ability to exchange views and to solve regulatory problems together. Modern technology may play a significant role here.

In an increasingly interconnected world, the understanding for legal problems that exist in other parts of the international community becomes more and more important. It therefore seems highly advisable to increase the interest and the competence of law students and practising lawyers in

---

43 The German Judiciary Act (Deutsches Richtergesetz) opens up that possibility when it defines the objectives of the areas of specialisation in German legal education: Section 5a, para. 2, explicitly includes the "the interdisciplinary and international bearing of the law" as a part of these specialised study programmes.

the field of comparative law. Once again, the question of skills and methods has a priority compared to the ability to solve a concrete case under a foreign legal regime. Supporting the view that the comparative law perspective does not only represent a specialised area of legal scholarship, but is also a part of legal methodology in general is not a new stance[44]. Indeed, the comparative method becomes indispensable in fields that are dealing with globalised legal problems. It goes beyond the mere use of comparative skills for interpreting a given domestic legal order and for predicting how legal problems will be solved there. Quite in contrast, the comparative method is helpful for understanding regulatory concepts in a broader perspective and for possibly improving the own domestic legal system. It remains indispensable, however, that the law students benefit from a sound legal education in their own domestic systems[45].

The comparative approach is furthermore fundamental to compromise-based solutions on the international level and, if applicable, in the European sphere. It is the basis for any intercultural exchange and awareness, which tend to become some of the major challenges in modern international legal science. That does not only apply to the traditional areas of comparative law, which, like contract or family law in particular, often lie within the field of private law, but it becomes relevant for basic constitutional choices as well[46]. Enhancing the status of the comparative method within the toolbox of legal methodology and improving the overall com-

---

44 See, prominently, Häberle, Peter, *Grundrechtsgeltung und Grundrechtsinterpretation im Verfassungsstaat – Zugleich zur Rechtsvergleichung als „fünfter" Auslegungsmethode*, JZ 1989, p. 913; id., Rechtsvergleichung im Kraftfeld des Verfassungsstaates: Methoden und Inhalte, Kleinstaaten und Entwicklungsländer, Berlin, Duncker und Humblot, 1992.

45 Indeed, I would defend this view more decidedly than Micklitz, Hans-Wolfgang, *The Bifurcation of Legal Education – National vs Transnational*, in: Gane, Christopher and Huang, Robin Hui (eds.), *Legal Education in the Global Context*, London and New York, Routledge, 2016, pp. 43, 59-60, who offers two alternatives, one of them consisting in diminishing the role of national law.

46 See, *e.g.* the approaches in European Union law concerning areas of coordination where the Union itself does not have any harmonising competences. A well-established example is the so-called European Semester regarding budgetary policies in the Member States: See article 2-a Council Regulation (EC) No 1466/97 of 7 July 1997 on the strengthening of the surveillance of budgetary positions and the surveillance and coordination of economic policies, consolidated version according to the Regulation (EU) No 1175/2011 of the European Parliament and of the Council of 16 November 2011, [2011] OJ L 306, p. 12. Furthermore, for an even more controversial field, *cf.* the recent approach of the European Commission regarding a rule of law monitoring in the Member States (Rule of Law Mecha-

parative legal skills seems to be an important part in preparing future lawyers in the best possible manner for the tasks that lie ahead of them. At the same time, it may add some methodological precision to the interdisciplinary debate on intercultural relations that will find itself in need of legal rationalisation if it intends to settle international disputes in a sustainable and non-discriminatory way. Legal education in general and law curricula in particular should therefore focus more on interdisciplinary and comparative aspects than they are doing it now.

## III. Improving linguistic competences

Improving linguistic competences is linked to the idea of a cultural exchange in legal studies and is a prerequisite for a serious comparative method. It is another field, which modern legal education should focus on. Hence, German law requires law faculties to include at least some minimum requirements for specialised language courses in their legal study programmes[47].

In rather general terms, the European Commission has formulated a further reaching perspective, which, however, can be transferred to the needs of modern legal studies in a globalised world[48]. It might provide a certain basis and guideline for an internationalised modern legal education and for study programmes even if they exceed the strict limits of European law and of the European single market.

In several initiatives and on different occasions[49], the Commission has highlighted the importance of multilingualism for economic, social,

---

nism): Communication from the Commission to the European Parliament, the European Council, the Council, the European Economic and Social Committee and the Committee of the Regions: *Strengthening the rule of law within the Union – A blueprint for action*, 17 July 2019, COM(2019) 343 final, p. 11.

47  Section 5a, para. 2, of the German Judiciary Act (Deutsches Richtergesetz) prescribes with relation to university studies that, apart from the compulsory subjects and areas of specialisation, "proof is required of the successful completion of a law course in a foreign language or a language course geared specifically to law". Obviously, this is a rather low standard as far as competences in the field of foreign languages are concerned. Nevertheless, it is a first important step in acknowledging the relevance of languages in legal education.

48  See, on this topic, Schwartze, Andreas, *A more European Legal Education – Lessons to be Learned*, in this volume, p. 67, with further references.

49  *Cf.* Sabatakakis, Ekaterini, *Vers une politique linguistique européenne? À propos de la communication de la Commission sur le multilinguisme et de la stratégie de Lisbonne,*

democratic, participatory, and cultural purposes. To that end, it has prepared a European framework strategy for multilingualism and the linguistic competences of the European citizens[50]. The ability to speak and to understand several different languages opens up the opportunity to not only
capture and explore a larger array of information, but also to connect with
more people in different countries and to improve one's own chances on
the international job market[51]. That does not only apply to the single market of the Union, but also to the competitive labour market for international lawyers dealing with transnational transactions or other topics in
different economic sectors. Regarding legal professions that are concerned
with law making tasks and international negotiations on diverse levels, the
command of different languages and hence the access to foreign legal cultures and traditional ways of reasoning will enhance the facilitation of
ideas and values that the lawyers have to convey and to represent in the relevant international exchange[52]. That applies primarily to those languages
which are widespread[53] and which are used in particularly influential legal
orders. However, for the purposes of an economic as well as of a cultural
and constitutional exchange, any language including those, which are less-

---

(2009) 530 RevMC 475, 482-483; De Witte, Bruno, *Language Law of the European
Union: Protecting or Eroding Linguistic Diversity?*, in: Craufurd Smith, Rachael (ed.),
*Culture and European Union Law*, Oxford, Oxford University Press, 2004, pp.
205-241.

50 See, *i.a.*, Communication from the Commission to the Council, the European
Parliament, the European Economic and Social Committee and the Committee
of the Regions: *A New Framework Strategy for Multilingualism*, 22 November 2005,
COM(2005) 596 final; Communication from the Commission to the Council:
*Framework for the European survey on language competences*, 13 April 2007,
COM(2007) 174 final; Communication from the Commission to the European
Parliament, the Council, the European Economic and Social Committee and the
Committee of the Regions: *Multilingualism: an asset for Europe and a shared com-
mitment*, 18 September 2008, COM(2008) 566 final; Communication from the
Commission to the European Parliament, the Council, the European Economic
and Social Committee and the Committee of the Regions: *Strengthening European
Identity through Education and Culture*, 14 November 2017, COM(2017) 673 final.

51 *Cf.* the communications from the Commission, COM(2008) 566 final, p. 3, 9, and
COM(2017) 673 final, p. 8. From the point of view of legal studies, see Meng-Papantoni, Maria, *The Teaching of Legal Practice in Europe: An Outlook*, in this volume, p. 119.

52 *Cf.*, for the European perspective, the Conclusions of the Council and of the Representatives of the Governments of the Member States, meeting within the Council, on the promotion of cultural diversity and intercultural dialogue in the external relations of the Union and its Member States, [2008] OJ C 320, pp. 10-2.

53 *Cf.* communication from the Commission, COM(2008) 566 final, p. 15.

widely used or which are just languages of neighbouring countries, is enriching and may open up paths for students, future employees or self-employed lawyers. In its so-called "Barcelona objectives", the European Union thus calls upon the European citizens to learn at least two languages besides their own mother tongue in which they will be able to communicate[54]. In an academic subject like law, which is heavily depending on communication and language, such a goal seems equally desirable and appropriate given the chances, which the knowledge of languages brings about.

This goal of an "individual multilingualism"[55], which the European institutions describe as an overall objective for the European market and for European citizens in general, entails a number of focal points and programmes that the Commission has designated[56] and that the Council has endorsed in several recommendations[57]. They contain a variety of measures in order to increase an active learning of languages at the various stages of education including life-long learning and mobility schemes. New digital technologies and the use of media play an increasingly important role as well. The parallels to modern legal education are apparent. Exchange programmes remain highly important elements in legal education and should be strengthened. Law faculties and legal study programmes should advertise them in an even more prominent manner and make them more attractive, *i.a.* by providing adequate means for accommodating incoming foreign students[58]. That implies taking into account the new opportunities which digitalisation brings about and which might significantly reduce the costs and efforts for an exchange online. Even though re-

---

54 Presidency conclusions of the Barcelona European Council, 15 and 16 March 2002, Part I, Doc. SN 100/02 ADD 1, para. 44; Council conclusions on language competences to enhance mobility, [2011] OJ C 372, p. 27; communications from the Commission, COM(2008) 566 final, p. 5, and COM(2005) 596 final, p. 4.

55 Sabatakakis, Ekaterini, *Vers une politique linguistique européenne? À propos de la communication de la Commission sur le multilinguisme et de la stratégie de Lisbonne*, (2009) 530 RevMC 475, 476.

56 See the communications from the Commission, COM(2005) 596 final, pp. 5-16; COM(2008) 566 final, pp. 7-15; COM(2017) 673 final, pp. 8, 15.

57 Council recommendations of 22 May 2019 on a comprehensive approach to the teaching and learning of languages, [2019] OJ C 189, p. 15, and of 22 May 2018 on key competences for lifelong learning, [2018] OJ C 189, p. 1, 8.

58 See, on this topic and with a view to cultural diversity, Evans, Carolyn, *Learning Opportunities in Multi-National Law School Classes: Potential and Pitfalls*, in: Gane, Christopher and Huang, Robin Hui (eds.), *Legal Education in the Global Context*, London and New York, Routledge, 2016, p. 61.

al life exchange programmes can never be fully compensated for by online programmes, these can, however, be supplementary in order to deepen the linguistic competences of students on a more regular basis. It does not seem to matter, for that purpose, whether the online elements rather connect with compulsory language courses or with substantive law courses, *e.g.* in the field of comparative law[59]. The options that a more digitalised teaching is offering are manifold and diverse with respect to the different areas in legal education where they can be implemented. The idea of bringing classes form different universities together, however, and thus of improving the opportunities for individual contacts between the students will not only meet with the language-related goals of modern legal education, but also with its overall objectives of cultural exchange.

## IV. Modern teaching methods

The following chapters in this volume intend to give an overview of a vast variety of modern teaching methods that are being discussed and applied nowadays. Indeed, legal education and its methods have always been a topic of interest in many jurisdictions. In the recent years, and notably in the times of the health crisis of 2020-21, not only the need for a significant change in the traditional ways of teaching has become apparent, but also the opportunities to implement and test new strategies and elements have increased considerably[60]. Probably not all the approaches that have been tested during the times of the pandemic will remain permanent parts of legal education in the future. Some experiments will vanish again or will be replaced by such traditional structures that have proven to be indispensable or superior compared to modern approaches. Given the specific characteristics of law and legal education[61], it seems inconceivable that in-person lectures with a structured and dogmatic approach can be replaced entirely by elements of distance learning which neither enable the students to really follow a holistic presentation of a field of law nor give them a comparable opportunity for critical exchange and questions.

The new elements in legal teaching therefore are meant to be improvements and additional proposals for better reaching out to the students and

---

59  See, *supra*, II.
60  See Balaguer Callejón, Francisco, *Modern Teaching Methods in European Legal Education*, in this volume, p. 53.
61  See, *supra*, A.I.

for communicating contents in a more accessible or effective manner. Modern teaching methods in legal education will be complementary and, of course, depend on the pedagogical abilities of the lecturer in question. Not every method will be suitable for everyone. Some of the elements are already widely accepted, but not yet a standard in every law curriculum. Some of them will be easy to implement in individual lectures, while others might require some more extensive changes as far as study guidelines and curricula are concerned. Legal education in its entirety will tend to become more complex and more sophisticated.

One can discern three different categories in terms of the main objectives of modern teaching methods that this volume will discuss, while an overlap is always possible.

## 1. *New technological opportunities*

The new methods partly relate to the new technological opportunities in the era of digitalisation. Distance learning, e-learning and virtual teaching[62] are nowadays highly efficient ways of making law and legal education accessible. These methods are not only matters of convenience or emergency solutions in times of crisis, but also encompass a social and participatory dimension. They do have their inherent limits as far as the classical ways of human and especially academic exchange are concerned. Furthermore, they require some new or additional guidance for the students as far as learning methods and learning resources are concerned[63]. In this context, video-based academic contributions[64] are directly linked to the digitalised ways of teaching. They are by no means a replacement for traditional academic writing. However, digitalisation is not restricted to textual forms. The claim of unity between academic research and academic teaching is suggesting a parallelism between digitalised teaching and research, yet always abiding by the same high academic standards.

---

62 Balaguer Callejón, Francisco, *Modern Teaching Methods in European Legal Education*, in this volume, p. 53; Guerra da Fonseca, Rui, *Distance Learning and Video-Based Academic Contributions: Steps Towards "A World Made New"?*, in this volume, p. 147.

63 Borman, Deborah L. and Haras, Catherine, *Something Borrowed: Interdisciplinary Strategies for Legal Education*, (2019) 68 Journal of Legal Education 357, 364-5.

64 Guerra da Fonseca, Rui, *Distance Learning and Video-Based Academic Contributions: Steps Towards "A World Made New"?*, in this volume, p. 147.

## 2. *Internationalised teaching*

Some of the new teaching methods concern the challenges of internationalised modern legal rules and the modern requirements in legal professions as far as languages and general key competences like presentation techniques are concerned. A traditional and widely accepted example are Moot Courts[65] that, however, are by no means compulsory in legal education all over the world. Especially the large international Moot Courts combine the training of different skills that can be extremely helpful for students in terms of their further career in different legal professions. Another safely established, but still rather modern example are law clinics, which have become more and more successful during the last decades, but which, obviously, require significant resources and commitment[66]. The tendency of internationalisation and the need of cross-border exchange not only and not even primarily in legal studies, but in a far more general way, has led the European Union to implement an initiative for so-called "European universities"[67]. It obviously stems from the idea of common European values and identity in education, but it could be, to a smaller extent, transferable to international cooperation in precisely defined fields of law as well.

---

65 Pereira da Silva, Vasco, *"My Fair Lady": Introductive Lecture*, in this volume, p. 41. See also, for an approach focussing on historical cases, Rigó, Balázs, *From the Student Circle of Playing Legal Cases through the Mentorprogramme to Social Responsibility*, in this volume, p. 157.

66 Hugg, Patrick R., *Perspectives from the United States: Pioneering in Legal Education as Innovation Advances*, in this volume, p. 129. See also, in this context, Thomas, Linden and Johnson, Nick, *The Clinical Legal Education Handbook*, London, University of London Press, 2020; Thomas, Linden, Vaughan, Steven, Malkani, Bharat, and Lynch, Theresa (eds.), *Reimagining Clinical Legal Education*, Oxford, Hart Publishing, 2018; Alemanno, Alberto and Khadar, Lamin, *Reinventing Legal Education. How Clinical Education Is Reforming the Teaching and Practice of Law in Europe*, Cambridge, Cambridge University Press, 2018; Wilson, Richard J., *The Global Evolution of Clinical Legal Education – More than a Method*, Cambridge, Cambridge University Press 2017.

67 Conclusions of the European Council meeting of 14 December2017, EUCO 19/1/17REV 1, p. 3. See also the European Commission website https:// ec.europa.eu/education/education-in-the-eu/european-education-area/european-universities-initiative_en (2.1.2021).

## 3. Students' specific needs in modern legal education

The final category aims at the specific needs and requirements of students in a modern world with an increasing degree of complexity[68]. Some teaching instruments concern psychological issues[69] sometimes connected with the ever increasing and sometimes overwhelming amount of substantive law content in legal education. Some elements of modern teaching tend to redefine the exchange between the lecturers and the students and are often based on new technological opportunities[70]. Examples are new learning activities with video and audio elements as well as new concepts like the "jigsaw classroom" or the "flipped classroom". Collaborative courses and team-based learning[71] are equally important elements that may improve the pedagogical toolbox in modern legal education and, at the same time, will create a readiness to formulate and defend legally founded positions and arguments in an international context. The same applies to student-led blogs under the supervision of lecturers or self-organised discussions in class with the opportunity of breakout sessions in order to prepare some preliminary tasks in groups[72]. While legal problems or fields that are particularly significant to students, as *e.g.* climate change law, are among the first choices for such approaches[73], they can be developed further into a

---

68 For an even further-reaching approach of a real gamification of certain elements in legal education, see Kathrani, Paresh, *The Gamification of Written Problem Questions in Law*, in: Devir, Catrina (ed.), *Modernising Legal Education*, Cambridge, Cambridge University Press, 2020, p. 186; Silverman, Gregory, *Law Games: The Importance of Virtual Worlds and Serious Video Games for the Future of Legal Education*, in: Rubin, Edward (ed.), *Legal Education in the Digital Age*, Cambridge, Cambridge University Press, 2012, p. 130.

69 Parashu, Dimitrios, *Is there an Optimal (and also Modern) Learning Method of Law in the Context of Educating International Lawyers?*, in this volume, p. 75.

70 See, on these topics, Kurti, Kersi, *Wording the Needs of Innovative Teaching in Law*, in this volume, p. 79; Jovanov, Kire, *'Jigsaw Classroom' and Law Teaching*, in this volume, p. 87; Künnecke, Arndt, *The Flipped Classroom Approach in Legal Education*, in this volume, p. 97; Hugg, Patrick R., *Perspectives from the United States: Pioneering in Legal Education as Innovation Advances*, in this volume, p. 129.

71 Hugg, Patrick R., *Perspectives from the United States: Pioneering in Legal Education as Innovation Advances*, in this volume, p. 129; Balsam, Jodi S., *Teaming Up to learn in the Doctrinal Classroom*, (2019) 68 Journal of Legal Education 261.

72 Pereira da Silva, Vasco, *"My Fair Lady": Introductive Lecture*, in this volume, p. 41.

73 Balsam, Jodi S., *Teaming Up to learn in the Doctrinal Classroom*, (2019) 68 Journal of Legal Education 261, 266.

project-based learning[74] that goes beyond the traditional concepts of case studies and seems particular appropriate for factually complex fields or, indeed, advanced and specialised courses in summer schools[75]. Involving the students' representatives[76] may be another worthwhile path in creating additional activities and making them available for law students while at the same time, keeping track of their expectations of a modern legal education.

## D. Conclusion

The challenges of modern structures of law as well as the factual situations that law has to address and to regulate necessitate several changes in legal education. The situation is nearly "gattopardesque": "Se vogliamo che tutto rimanga come è, bisogna che tutto cambi"[77] – "If we want everything to remain as it is, everything needs to change." In order to remain relevant and to fulfil its tasks in the interest of the law and of those who are going to be future lawyers, legal education needs to change and to adapt to the new world. At the same time, it is necessary to retain such elements of legal education that have proven to be adequate and useful to deliver the results which society is expecting from law.

That, however, does not answer the question of which changes seem reasonable and beneficial. The contributions in this volume might provide some form of direction with a particular view to modern teaching methods. Concluding the broad outline of both the current challenges and the potential instruments leads us back to the question of what the mission of university education in general and of legal education in particular should consist in.

Modern legal education has to offer new and improved paths for law students in order to enable them to enter the labour market successfully. It

---

74 See, by way of example and in more detail, Carpenter, Anna, *Developing 'NextGen' Lawyers through Project-Based Learning*, in: Devir, Catrina (ed.), *Modernising Legal Education*, Cambridge, Cambridge University Press, 2020, p. 126.

75 For a "field-based approach", Börk, Karrigan and Burmeister, Kurtis, *Cases and Places: A Field-Based Approach to Teaching Natural Resource and Environmental Law*, (2019) 68 Journal of Legal Education 261.

76 See Rigó, Balázs, *From the Student Circle of Playing Legal Cases through the Mentor-programme to Social Responsibility*, in this volume, p. 157; Kurti, Kersi, *Wording the Needs of Innovative Teaching in Law*, in this volume, p. 79.

77 Giuseppe Tomasi di Lampedusa, *Il Gattopardo*, Milan, Feltrinelli (1st edition 1958), 27th edition 1978, p. 21.

has to provide guidance and to keep an eye on the requirements of modern legal professions in order to increase the employability of law students. In doing so, it has to respect their capacities, which means that structure normally will outdo specialisation. Within this framework, modern legal education has to focus on competences concerning comparative methods, interdisciplinary contacts[78] and international exchange. Languages and mobility programmes[79] become more and more important. Increasing the exchange with other faculties by way of online tools is a highly desirable new feature.

As a part of academic studies, however, legal education has to pursue and to enshrine the core elements that have been constituting the university and the academic world for the last decades and centuries. Thus, the relevance of academics freedoms remains unreservedly essential in modern legal education. Despite all new methods and instruments, the effective use of those freedoms has to be secured. Equally, fundamental values[80] play an outstanding role. Even though, in a globalised world, it might not always be easy to define a fixed set of common values, the rule of law and the respect for human rights are indispensable. Besides that, the general academic values such as openness and critical thinking, respect and honesty in the academic discourse are by no means less important in modern legal education than they used to be in any traditional concept of university studies. These values have to remain the core features of modern legal education, even if everything else might be changing.

---

78 See, in more detail, the contribution of Pereira da Silva, Vasco, *"My Fair Lady"*: *Introductive Lecture*, in this volume, p. 41.

79 Regarding the example of the ELPIS network and the corresponding programmes, see the introductory remarks by Oppermann, Bernd H., *Initial Thoughts about ELPIS*, in this volume, p. 35.

80 Balaguer Callejón, Francisco, *Modern Teaching Methods in European Legal Education*, in this volume, p. 53; on the topic of values in international legal education, see also Sampford, Charles and Breakey, Hugh, *Law, Lawyering and Legal Education. Building an ethical profession in a globalizing world*, London and New York, Routledge, 2017; Ferris, Graham, *Uses of Values in Legal Education*, Cambridge, Antwerp and Portland, Intersentia, 2015, especially Ch. 3 ("The Content of a Value-Informed Curriculum"); Redmond, Paul, *The Values Dimension of Legal Education: Educating for Justice and Service*, in: Gane, Christopher and Huang, Robin Hui (eds.), *Legal Education in the Global Context*, London and New York, Routledge, 2016, p. 99.

# Initial Thoughts about ELPIS
# Eingangsgedanken zu ELPIS

*Bernd H. Oppermann*[*]

Since we have always practiced English for use of our network language, you may wonder why I was starting in German tongue. Indeed, I believe that the Dean, addressing public representatives should do this in a native tone. After all, the Mayor of the City of Hanover and the Vice President Prof. von Haaren are present, and our new Lord Mayor is aware of the recent occasion as well as of the existence of your network. Even if I might have decided otherwise on the choice of language, different from France, it would not be a crime under German law. However, one unique element of the programmes connected to this cooperation, are its language schemes. Moreover, an important point of entering the excellence class of ERASMUS MUNDUS, once upon a time, was the dual language and mobility scheme of our products.

I am not a translator; therefore, I shall spare out the translation of my German opening remarks into English language. Let me give you an animated version thereof: Finally, we were independent enough to shift the organizer and chairman of the network positions. This counts for the regional sphere, as in Hanover, after Professor Hilmar Fenge and myself; you are confronted with the third generation of responsibility in the person of Professor Germelmann. Some time ago, we had even managed the shift of the organisational shell at Lisbon as we performed the almost impossible task of changing the partner institution under a vivid European scheme, as the circumstances had required doing so. This counts even more for the European level where we have managed to shift the chairman and the organisation of the network itself, later of its most valuable European educational products from Hanover to Lisbon as the circumstances had required doing so. Even more, I always liked the idea that we managed to keep partner re-

[*] Prof. Dr. Dr. h.c. (Rouen) Bernd H. Oppermann, Prof. h.c. (UMCS), LL.M. (UCLA), Gottfried Wilhelm Leibniz University of Hanover (Chair for German, European and International Civil and Commercial Law).

lations under unfavourable conditions and were able to vitalize at later state, although, for the UK partner institutions solely, this scheme did not really work out. I just hope, that the circumstances do not worsen so much that we need to move sensitive things further away, as once the royal court of Portugal had done by shifting its temporary residence to Brazil.

What has brought our institutions and predecessors together was a common European project – more than the old MLE Master program – in order to re-establish European space for higher education even for the law faculties which, beyond common Roman Law tradition, were subject of many regional influences. For the founding generation – Professor Hilmar Fenge – a post war motivation was additionally virulent. To conserve and spread such common European goods, we have employed EU-schemes as ERASMUS, ERASMUS MUNDUS, TEMPUS and others, thereby not excluding non-EU members as Norway, Turkey, Russia, or Switzerland. I have noticed that the next ELPIS conference is planned to take place at the University of Fribourg, Switzerland.

However, the former ELPIS programme and network experienced challenge by a common TEMPUS project, which brought a few of our members together with Russian universities. Even more workload brought the LL.M. joint degree as we became a pioneer project member of the new ERASMUS MUNDUS scheme und were directly confronted with the demands of the EU Commission. Designed as real European joint degree of the Faculties of Law of the Universities of Hanover, Lisbon, Rouen, and Le Havre, the latter was substituted by Vilnius at Lithuania. The 2-year master degree „LL.M. Eur" was meant to be a pioneer scheme of European education, one of only 19 throughout the European Union. The legal and cultural skills were arranged to correspond with a specific mobility and specific continental languages. Meanwhile, quite a few of our programme students proved to be very successful in science, business and administration. A further challenge imposed on us by the EU Commission directly, was that we had to include higher educational institutions of other regions of the earth at Brazil, China, India, Thailand and Vietnam, not to forget loose connections to institutions of the United States of America. The acquaintance and teachings with students, the fruitful teamwork with visiting lecturers, the partners of the Consortium, the European Community and last but not least with the helpful professors and all the supporting friends of this program has turned out to be very interesting and inspiring. Some of the other projects I have mentioned before in German language only briefly were our book publications whether collectively in meanwhile 4 volumes, or individually by specific research works, by conference publications or joint European Ph.D. dissertations. It remains to point out another of our traditional scientific conferences on European legal education, as it will take place on Saturday.

My warm welcome to you at the Guest House of Leibniz University Hanover in the name of the Faculty of Law. It is a pleasure for me, regardless of the imaginative hat I actually wear, or the institutional role I actually have to carry out.

Im Namen der Fakultät darf ich Sie von ganzem Herzen willkommen heißen.

Das gilt für unsere internationalen Gäste ebenso wie für die einheimischen Besucher. Es handelt sich um ein ELPIS Netzwerk-Treffen, unser europäisches Fakultätsnetzwerk, welches an wechselnden Orten so oft stattfand, dass wir mittlerweile das Zählen aufgegeben haben. Auch in Hannover haben wir viel getagt, so dass sich eine gewisse lokale Präferenz feststellen lässt.

Seitens der Fakultät legen wir großen Wert auf unsere Auslandsaktivitäten, mit denen wir uns vor vielen anderen juristischen Fakultäten – das ist die Vergleichsgröße – ausgezeichnet haben und nach wie vor auszeichnen. Auch wenn die Juristische Fakultät der Leibniz Universität erst gut 45 Jahre zählt – im besten Alter ist, sozusagen – kann man von einer Tradition reden, bei der uns die Stadt Hannover und die Leibniz Universität, hier insb. das International Office und gelegentlich auch das Land Niedersachsen unterstützt haben. Ich erinnere mich etwa an die 50-Jahresfeier des Elysee-Vertrages, zu der, da die Haute Normandie nicht nur Partnerregion von Niedersachsen, sondern die Stadt Rouen auch Partnerstadt Hannovers ist, wir mit einer mehrphasigen deutsch-französischen Veranstaltung die schönsten Räume des Rathauses nutzen durften. Auch mit einzelnen Akteuren ebenso aus den Landesministerien wie aus dem Landtag hat die Zusammenarbeit stets gut funktioniert. Repräsentativ möchte ich unter jenen den neuen Oberbürgermeister, Herrn Belit Onay nennen, der ein Absolvent unserer Juristischen Fakultät ist.

Als tradiert darf man das Rechtsfakultäten-Netzwerk ELPIS bezeichnen, weil mittlerweile Herr Professor Germelmann bereits in dritter Generation hierfür Verantwortung zeichnet. Gegründet worden war die internationale Kooperation vor rund 35 Jahren von Herrn Kollegen Fenge, der es 16 Jahre betreute und entwickelte, darauf folgte ich selber, nunmehr wiederum sind es seit einigen Jahren Herr Germelmann für die deutsche Seite, Professor Pereira da Silva für die europäische.

Inhaltlich ging es zunächst, aber nicht nur um europäische Netzwerkpflege zwecks individuellen Austauschs von Studierenden, jungen WissenschaftlerInnen und Professoren unter den EU-Förderschemata ERASMUS; ERASMUS MUNDUS und TEMPUS sowie um Förderungen durch den DAAD, durch Humboldt und weitere Förderwerke. Arbeit bereitet auch die Etablierung und Durchführung zweier juristischer Studiengänge, nämlich einem europäischen *LL.M. joint degree* zwischen vieren unserer Partner, sowie einem ehemaligen Magisterstudiengang, welcher derzeit als Zertifikatsstudiengang der LUH in Zusammenarbeit mit zeitweise 36 europäischen Partnern fungiert. Im Hinblick auf jene Studiengänge gab es eine Reihe gemeinsamer, teils üppiger zeremonieller Graduiertenfeiern. Bei ELPIS geht es weiter um die Planung, Beantragung und Durchführung gemeinsamer Projekte. Dazu gehören gemeinsame Buchpublikationen, oft Sammelwerke, aber auch die Förderung europäischer Promotionen. Auch werden regelmäßig gemeinsame Tagungen veranstaltet, welche nunmehr häufiger in Verbindung mit den Netzwerktreffen durchgeführt werden. So hat dies Herr Kollege Germelmann auch für die aktuelle Konferenz vorgesehen, sodass wir den Ereignissen insgesamt dreier Tage erwartungsvoll entgegenblicken dürfen.

Damit sind indessen die internationalen Aktivitäten unserer Rechtsfakultät keineswegs erschöpft. Verfügen wir doch über zwei weitere Internationale Bachelor- und Masterstudiengänge im Bereich des IT-Rechts, über ein VIS Moot Court Team, weitere internationale Moot Courts, zwei Rechtskliniken sowie nicht zuletzt über im europäischen und internationalen Bereich profilierte Lehrstühle. Mit diesem Hinweis mag es sein Bewenden haben; denn heute geht es ausschließlich um die ELPIS-Delegiertentagung mit anschließender Fachkonferenz.

Zum Abschluss des deutschsprachigen Teils der Tagungseröffnung durch den Dekan nehme ich die Gelegenheit gerne wahr, mich bei der Vertreterin des Präsidiums unseres Institution, Frau Vizepräsidentin für Auslandsangelegenheiten der Leibniz Universität Hannover, Frau von Haaren, und dem Herrn Bürgermeister der Stadt Hannover, Herrn Herrmann, im Namen der Fakultät für die Aufwertung unserer Veranstaltung durch Ihre geschätzte Präsenz zu bedanken.

# "My Fair Lady": Introductive Lecture

*Vasco Pereira da Silva**

## A. *Theoretical approach to Law Teaching*

> *Eliza – The rain in Spain stays mainly in the plain.*
> *Prof. Higgins – Again.*
> *Eliza – The rain in Spain stays mainly in the plain.*

I begin saying that it is for me a great honour and pleasure to moderate the first Panel of our Conference, with the promising title: «Modern Teaching Methods in European Legal Education. Moving Towards a "European Education Area». I would like also to add that this is a renewed pleasure, since I share this table with two old friends: Professor Balaguer Callejón (from the University of Granada), my accomplice in countless scientific adventures; and Dr. Christoph Bouyssi (from the Leibniz University of Hannover), regular partner at the conferences I attend in Hannover.

As moderator, it is up to me to provoke and comment on the interventions of the other participants in this panel, which I will do with great joy. I begin with a (very) short introduction inspired by the film «My Fair Lady», directed by George Cuckor (based in the play "Pygmalion", written by George Bernard Shaw), with a leading couple of actors: Audrey Hepburn as Eliza Doolittle, and Rex Harrison as Prof. Henry Higgins, that I entitled «"My Fair Lady": Introductive Lecture».

At the beginning of the film we watch the arrogance of Prof. Higgins (a Phonetics expert) teaching a girl picked up on the street because of a bet he made about being able to turn a poor girl into a great lady throughout education, while Eliza (a cockney flower girl) was bored and indifferent to the lesson. By the second part of the film, we saw Eliza's openness and availability to learn and the efforts of Prof. Higgins not to give in to the passion that begins to emerge between the two of them. And we learn from the movie that every learning relationship should turn into a love relation.

---

* Prof. Dr. Dr. h.c. (Hannover) Vasco Pereira da Silva, Professor of the Law Faculty of the University of Lisbon (Professor Catedrático da Faculdade de Direito da Universidade de Lisboa).

41

Like Professor Higgins also a Law Professor needs to combine research and teaching. The Law professor is required to know how to independently investigate and construct his thinking in the domain of his own legal discipline, as he must also be required to be able to communicate, to bring the fruit of his doctrinal work to the students, that is to say that he should be able to teach[1]. Law teaching poses specific pedagogical problems, since it is a scientific domain whose object is a reality that is intended to be applied, which imposes the need to attend to the inseparable relationship between science and legal technique, between the norm and the reality, between "law in the books" and "law in action"[2].

Nowadays, overcoming the classical dichotomy that separated exclusively theoretical and "bookish" teaching methods of law (corresponding to the Roman-Germanic model), on the one hand, and exclusively practical and vocational methods (corresponding to the Anglo-Saxon model), on the other hand, we are witnessing a tendency towards the combination of both methods of law teaching. This new methodological approach, mixing theory and practice, combining law science and technique, seems to be particularly suited to the complexity of today's legal phenomena and it is an inevitable consequence of the "Europeanization" and the "globalization" of the Law.

In my view, we should also not separate teaching from the nature of the Law[3]. Therefore we can' t forget that between law and culture there is a kind of "loving relationship" (to quote a phrase aptly coined by MICHEL PRIEUR when describing the relationship between law and aesthetics[4]), in which each of them "completes" the other, with advantages and benefits for both insofar as "culture forces law to evolve and law rewards it by making it more universal and democratic"[5]. The fruits of that loving relationship are, on one hand, the "culture of law", i.e. the view of law as a cultural phenomenon asking to be interpreted and analysed according to the

---

1 Pereira da Silva, Vasco, *Ensinar Direito (a Direito) – Contencioso Administrativo*, Almedina, Coimbra, 1989, p. 12.

2 Pereira da Silva, Vasco, *Ensinar Verde a Direito – Estudo de Metodologia do Ensino do Direito do Ambiente (em "Ambiente de Bolonha")*, Almedina, Coimbra, 2006.

3 Pereira da Silva, Vasco, *A Cultura a que Tenho Direito. Direitos Fundamentais e Cultura*, Almedina, Coimbra, 2007, p. 14/25.

4 Prieur, Michel, *Préface*, in: Makowiak, Jessica, *Esthétique et Droit*, L.G.D.J., Paris, 2004, p. V.

5 Prieur, Michel, *Préface*, cit., in: Makowiak, Jessica, *Esthétique et D.*, cit., p. VI.

methodology(ies) of "cultural studies" (HÄBERLE)[6]; on the other, cultural law, the study of cultural phenomena employing legal research methodologies (of the different branches of law).

The need for a cultural framework for legal phenomena and the consequent adoption of scientific methodologies of an interdisciplinary nature has also of late been supported and emphasized by current visions of law as a "literary genre" ("law as literature"), or "as musical expression") ("law as music"), or even "as dramatic art" (law as performative art"). This is typical of modern trends in legal philosophy such as the so-called "critical theory" ("critical legal studies") or the "post-modern notion of law" ("postmodern jurisprudence") (see WHITE, DOUZINAS, WARRINGTON, MCVEIGH, WARD, MINDA, LUEDERSSEN, LEVINSON, BALKIN)[7], that endeavour to "understand law – and its various planes of objectivation and realisation – making use of a determinative analogy with the creative, interpretive and communication processes employed in literary discourse (and the same applies to other artistic expressions as music, theatre, opera, cinema) and in the "retextualization" exercises set off by it (AROSO LINHARES)[8].

---

6  Häberle, Peter, *Verfassungslehre als Kulturwissenschaft (Schriften zum öffentlichen Recht)*, Duncker & Humblot, Berlin, 1998, *Teoria de la Constitución como Ciencia de la Cultura*, Tecnos, Madrid, 2000, p. 71.

7  Boyd White, James, *Heracles' Bow. Essays on the Rhetoric and Poetics of the Law*, University of Wisconsin Press, Madison, 1985; *Justice as Translation. An Essay in Cultural and Legal Criticism*, The University of Chicago Press, Chicago, 1990; *The Edge of Meaning*, University of Chicago Press, Chicago, 2001; Douzinas, Costas / Warrington, Ronnie / McVeigh, Susan, *Postmodern Jurisprudence – The Law of Text in the Texts of the Law*, Routledge, London / New York, 1991; Ward, Ian, *Law and Literature*, in: Law and Critique ("Springer Philosophy of Law Journal"), volume IV, n.º 1, 1993, p. 43; *Introduction to Critical Legal Theory*, 2nd ed., Cavendish Publishing, London / Sidney / Portland, Oregon, 2004; Minda, Gary, *Postmodern Legal Movements: Law and Jurisprudence at Century's End*, New York University Press, New York, 1995; Luederssen, Klaus, *Produktive Spiegelungen: Recht in Literatur, Theater und Film*, 2nd ed., Nomos, Baden-Baden, 2002; Levinson, Sanford / Balkin, J. M., *Law, Music and other Performing Arts*, in «University of Pennsylvania Law Review», volume n.º 139, 1991, p. 1597; Balkin, J. M., *Cultural Software: A Theory of Ideology*, Yale University Press, Yale, 1998; Balkin, J. M. / Levinson, Sanford, *Law and Performance*, in http://www.yale.edu/lawweb/jbalkin/articles/london21.htm, p. 1; Balkin, J. M. / Levinson, Sanford, *Interpreting Law and Music: Performance Notes on "The Banjo Serenader" and "The Lying Crowd of Jews"*, in «Cardozo Law Review», n.º 20, 1999, p. 1513.

8  Aroso Linhares, Jose M., *Entre a Reescrita Pós-Moderna da Juridicidade e o Tratamento Normativo da Diferença ou a Prova como um Exercício de "Passagem" nos Limites da Juridicidade (Imagens e Reflexos Pré-Metodológicos deste Percurso)*, in: «Boletim da Faculdade de Direito da Universidade de Coimbra – Studia Juridica», Coimbra, 2001, p.

It is, however, also interesting to see how "the new" meets "the old" considering that the dimension of law as a cultural science has deep roots and a long historical tradition, namely in the Middle Ages, when not only did the teaching of law occur according to a rationale of "cultural integration", combining the study of sciences and arts (the *trivium* and the *quadrivium*), but the interpretation and enactment of legal rules was deeply influenced by contributions from the world of arts and literature.[9]

The vision of law as a "literary genre" springs from the notion that the jurists' foremost mission is to interpret the rules to be applied and this involves a prior analysis of all the possible meanings and (historical, current and future) contexts of the "text", in a manner very similar to the way in which literary theoreticians or critics appreciate the different "readings" of the "work", identifying location and time period. Bringing the tasks of jurists and literary professionals closer (but also the position of individuals with regard to legal rules and of readers vis-à-vis literary works) is instrumental in overcoming the "quarrel of methods" and leads to a search for the "universality of the hermeneutical aspect" (GADAMER).[10]

Hence the assertion that "we have to read law as a kind of literature and have to read literature as a kind of law" (BOYD WHITE).[11] The reason is that the interpretation of rules should not correspond to "a rather mechanical institutional system", in which the lawyer resorts to formalism, whose sole concern is "efficiency of operation, rather than taking on the "creative task" of "confronting the realities of human experience and of talking about it, and of shaping it, in language" (BOYD WHITE).[12] The role of the lawyer consists, therefore, in dealing with social "archetypes", drafting a kind of "narrative" for a concrete community of people, which can be described as " a group of people who tell a shared story in a shared language" (BOYD WHITE).[13]

---

60; *O Logos da Juridicidade sobre o Fogo Cruzado do Ethos e do Pathos – Da Convergência com a Literatura (Law as Literature) à Analogia com uma Poiêsis-Technê de Realização ("Law as Musical and Dramatic Performance")*, in: «Boletim da Faculdade de Direito – Universidade de Coimbra», volume LXXX, Coimbra, 2004, p. 59.

9 De Albuquerque, Ruy, *Para uma Revisão da Ciência Jurídica Medieval: a Integração da Autorictas Poética no Discurso dos Juristas (Ars Inveniendis)*, in «Revista da Faculdade de Direito da Universidade de Lisboa», vol. XLIII, n.º 2, 2002, p. 935.

10 Gadamer, Hans-Georg, *Verité et Méthode – Les Grandes Lignes d'une Herméneutique Philosophique* (trad.), Éditions du Seuil, Paris, 10976, p. 11.

11 Boyd White, James, *Heracles' B. E. on the R. and P. of the L.*, cit., p. 122, 123.

12 Boyd White, James, *The Edge of M.*, cit., p. 222.

13 Boyd White, James, *Heracles' B. E. on the R. and P. of the L.*, cit., pp. 173 e 175.

However, law "exists to be applied". It is, therefore, necessary that the "text" corresponds to the "reality" of life. Thus, like the "translator" whose job consists in putting a text in "another language" in such a way that it keeps its original meaning – and, as much as possible, a similar formal configuration – in its new linguistic codification, the judge will also match rules and facts, connecting both within the (always) "new" context of the application of the law. "To say what the law is in a specific case is, therefore, to match the "language of the rules" with the "language of society". It is this that binds lawyers and translators making possible to speak of "justice as translation" (BOYD WHITE)[14].

From literature to music ("law as music") and to dramatic art ("law as performative art"), the comparison between legal and cultural phenomena makes it possible to emphasize the creative role of the "entire community". Hence the trend to look for an "analogy with the "interpretive arts" ("performing arts") – "music and drama- and with the "communities and institutions" that perform them, replacing the "study of law as literature by the broader study of law as performing art" (BALKIN / LEVINSON)[15].

And this for two reasons: in the first place, because "law on the books" and "the social practice of law" are two different things, just as music on a sheet is not the same as the social practice of music. Law and music involve the transformation of the ink on a sheet into the behaviour of people ("enacted behaviour of others"). In reality, there exists only "law" (or music or drama) in action, as opposed to poetry or fiction, the texts of which do not require a "performance", but can be silently read by each individual (BALKIN / LEVINSON)[16]. When "interpreting" legal rules, "operating" the transformation of "legislated law" into "law in action", the jurist plays a unique and creative role, that of determining which law is applicable to concrete situations of life. In the second place, "just as music and theatre, law occurs in front of a public audience, towards which the interpreter/ performer carries specific responsibilities. The interpreters – legal, musical, theatrical – "must persuade others that the conception of the work put before them is, in some sense, authoritative"). And no matter whether the performance is convincing or not, it produces effects on the audience"

---

14 Boyd White, James, *Justice as T. An E. in C. and L. C.*, cit. pp. 229.
15 Balkin, J. M. / Levinson, Sanford, *Law and P.*, cit., in http://www.yale.edu/lawweb /jbalkin/articles/london21.htm, cit., p. 1. See Balkin, J. M. / Levinson, Sanford, *Interpreting L. and M.: P. N. on "The B. S." and "The L. C. of J."*, cit., in «Cardozo L. R.», cit., pp. 1513 e ss.
16 Balkin, J. M. / Levinson, Sanford, *Law and P.*, cit., in http://www.yale.edu/lawweb /jbalkin/articles/london21.htm, cit., p. 1.

(BALKIN / LEVINSON)[17]. That is why the jurist's interpretation, despite being unique and creative, corresponds to the externalization of a norm and it acquires thereby an unavoidable dimension of "publicity", typical of modern "technical mass societies" (ROGÉRIO SOARES)[18]. In particular, in what concerns the judge, the "artistic performance" carried out by the "interpreter" produces simultaneously legal and *de facto* effects since, on one hand, it regulates the legal situation of the case at hand while having, at the same time, an impact on the entire legal system; and, on the other it has immediate effect both on the cases before court and on the life of society.

Bringing the "art of law" closer to other artistic and cultural manifestations may be carried out in multiple ways. For my part, I have not only attempted to use a legal discourse capable of establishing an ongoing dialogue with the arts and literature[19], but also carry out a few scientific and pedagogic experiences, as for instance:

- an approach to "law as cooking": in the course of a pedagogical experience that I usually undertake with my students of "Administrative law", where I explain the discretionary power of the administration by elaborating a (virtual) recipe. It consists in choosing a recipe (a different one each year), in order to illustrate all the steps needed for the Administration ("cook") to apply the rules ("recipes") to the concrete case ("dish"). This goes from reading and interpreting the rule ("recipe") to making the decision ("dish"), by way of the selection of the relevant facts, the establishment of proceedings ("choice and buying of the ingredients"), the assessment and composition of the interests at issue ("mixing and combining the ingredients"). In order to demonstrate that at each stage there exists "a margin of appreciation" (for example "to cook in a bain marie", "to fry until golden") and "a degree of discretion" (for instance to salt and pepper according to taste"), depending on "choices" for which the Administration ("the cook") is responsible. These choices, in some cases, depend solely on the relative merits of the decision ("better or worse preparation of the dish"), in other, more serious ones, they give rise to an illegality of the decision (for instance "a burnt dish", "food poisoning"). In fact, the creative power of the Administration –

---

17 Balkin, J. M. / Levinson, Sanford, *Law and P.*, cit., in http://www.yale.edu/lawweb /jbalkin/articles/london21.htm, cit., p. 1.

18 Soares, Rogério, *Direito Público e Sociedade Técnica*, Atlântida, Coimbra, 1969.

19 Pereira da Silva, Vasco, *Em Busca do Acto Administrativo Perdido*, Almedina, Coimbra, 1996.

and the same applies, *mutatis mutandis,* to the actions of the cook – "may concern either the determination of the meaning of the law, or, simultaneously, the choice of how to behave in that context. No rupture occurs between these two operations (of realisation of the law), but there is rather continuity. Consequently, the degree of discretion is not an extra-juridical reality but something that grafts itself on the process of reconstitution consisting in the interpretation and application of law"[20];

- an understanding of "law as cinema", analysing" law in movies" and "movies in law" (GREENFIELD / OSBORN / ROBSON)[21]. An approach of "law as cinema" that has to do with both the doctrinal and the pedagogical perspective and that arises from the use of "law movies" as an object and an instrument of the teaching of law. Something I attempt when I use "environmental law movies" in my courses on environmental law[22], as well as I am doing right now using «My Fair Lady» to talk about pedagogy of law;

- a vision of "law as psychoanalysis", which results from the concept of law as a "cultural science", relying in this specific case on the methods of "cultural psychoanalysis" (but it is also possible to use the methods of any other science, in particular of cultural sciences). This is what I sought to do when I analysed the evolution of administrative justice in Portugal over the years, reconciling the administrative process and psychoanalysis, with the purpose of creating the right conditions for its urgent doctrinal renovation. To that end, I had to put administrative justice through cultural psychoanalysis sessions, so as to enable the traumatic facts to be remembered – first the older ones, with the patient sitting on the couch of history, and, afterwards, the more recent, sitting also the patient on the couch of the constitution and of Europe – and

---

20  Pereira da Silva, Vasco, *Verde Cor de Direito. Lições de Direito do Ambiente*, Almedina, Coimbra, 2002, p. 78, 79. V; *Em Busca do Acto Administrativo Perdido*, Almedina, Coimbra, 1996, p. 85.

21  Greenfield, Steve / Osborn, Guy / Robson, Peter, *Film and the Law*, Cavendish Publishing, London / Sidney, 2001. See also Presno Linera, Miguel Ángel / Rivaya, Benjamin, *Una Introducción Cinematográfica al Derecho*, Tirant lo Blanch, Valência, 2006.

22  Pereira da Silva, Vasco, *Ensinar Verde a Direito. Metodologia do Ensino do Direito do Ambiente (em "Ambiente de Bolonha")*, Almedina, Coimbra, 2006, p. 237.

to achieve a catharsis, thus helping administrative process to face the realities of the present in a healthy manner"[23].

The truth is that numberless combinations are useful and desirable, in an endless array of possible harmonisation, convergence and hybridization of cultural and legal perspectives[24]. This cultural approach to the law seems to me as being the right way to face also legal methodology.

Like Prof. Higgins, I also have my "tricks": I use some methodological exercises in Law teaching. It is now the time to show you three of the pedagogical experiences I use to teach my Courses: the Blog, the (organized) Discussion of a controversial theme, and (my model of) Moot Court, Trial Simulation, or "mock court"

## B. *The Blog*

**Eliza – In Hertford, Hereford, and Hampshire, hurricanes hardly ever happen.**
**Higgins – Again.**
**Eliza – In Hertford, Hereford, and Hampshire, hurricanes hardly ever happen.**

In the first lecture of every Course I teach I challenge the students to create a Blog, Responsible for this task, is a group of volunteers (3 to 5 persons) that will take care of the design and of the creation of the blog in the internet, as well as to send an invitation to each student of the Course and to the Professor and his team, all of them becoming the status of "authors".

After the blog is created all the students should participate in several ways according to their choices:

- discussion of complex issues seen from different perspectives,
- case studies resolution,
- writing of research essays on topics previously investigated,
- creation of a kind of "analysis laboratory" of the daily legal reality, where they should comment from a law point of view the controversial cases there are news in the media,

---

23 See Pereira da Silva, Vasco, *O Contencioso Administrativo no Divã da Psicanálise. Ensaio sobre as Acções no Novo Processo Administrativo*, Almedina, Coimbra, 2005, p. 5.
24 Pereira da Silva, Vasco, *A Cultura a que Tenho Direito. Direitos Fundamentais e Cultura*, cit., p. 14/25.

- jurisprudence commentaries,
- discussion on law-making procedure.

This blog exercise is an appropriate way for developing and testing the written skills of the students, as well as a reliable instrument of assessments, since it contains written elements of a "continuous evaluation system".

## C. The (organized) Discussion of a controversial theme

*Eliza – How kind of you to let me come.*
*Prof. Higgins – Again.*
*Eliza – How kind of you to let me come.*

Previously, the students are organized in 2 teams (from 5 to 7 elements), each group choosing to defend one of the controversial positions under discussion. Then, each team will present their own position, in the next lecture, face to face with the opposing team, discussing the advantages of the position they have to defend, answering the questions raised by the other team and contesting the arguments in question.

The scheme of the intervention of each team in the debate is predefined. It goes like this:

- initial allegations for the submission of the position defended, with a preliminary presentation of the main arguments (5 minutes for each team),
- 3 successive intervention periods for each of the teams to raise questions and to criticise the arguments of the opponent team as well as to answer to the opponents' objections (3 times, 3 minutes per period, for each team),
- each team needs to deal with a period of questions made by all the other students in the audience (10 minutes maximum for both teams),
- final allegations, for the presentation of the closing arguments (5 minutes for each team).

The Professor must ensure the scrupulous compliance of the times by each team and the respect of the rules of a healthy discussion. in the end, there will be a vote to determine who won the debate (with the participation of all the students with the exclusion of the team members). After having voted who was the best team, it is also possible to vote on which position the students like best or agree more (having both a "formal" and a "substantial" vote on the topic in question).

This is an excellent exercise for testing the oral skills of the students. And, at the same time, it is an interesting way of training the skills necessary to the exercise of the law professions by a game competition. But it can also become a way for testing written skills if you ask the students to resume (and comment) the main arguments of each team and to put them in the blog (we described just now in the previous exercise).

### D. (My model of) Moot court, trial simulation, or "mock court"

> *Eliza – Cup of tea.*
> *Prof. Higgins – Cup-of-tea. And then say: cup-cup-cup-of-of-of; cup-cup-cup-of-of-of...*
> *Eliza – Cup-cup-cup-of-of-of; cup-cup-cup-of-of-of...*

Being able to act like a legal professional (judge, lawyer, public prosecutor), as well as playing the role of a witness in a simulated court, is one of the best exercises I know in order to learn how "law in action" works, after having studied the "law in the books". My personal "recipe" for a trial simulation or a moot court, needs the following ingredients:

- 1 team of judges (5 students)
- 1 team to represent each of the parts (7 to 10 students each, including 2 to 4 witnesses for each party)
- 1 team of the Public Prosecutor (3 to 5 students, that may also include 2 witnesses if required)
- Journalists to write and comment the judgement may also exist, or a court clerk, like in the "real life".

The "recipe" is made in 2 steps – or, if you prefer, a different approach and a change on the metaphor: the "game" takes place in 2 sessions:
1st (Step) Session – Audience of Judgment

- the team of judges rules the audience, from the beginning to the end of the judgement,
- each theme does a brief presentation of his case (namely pointing out the relevant facts),
- each team presents 2 to 4 witnesses (that prepared the statement together with the lawyers of his part),
- the witnesses are questioned and counter-questioned by each part (and the judge),
- each part presents closing arguments,
- the team of judges put an end to the trial.

2nd (Step) Session – Reading of the Court decision

- next week, the judges formally read the full sentence,
- the defeated part may appeal, indicating summarily his own arguments,
- in the end, the parts publish in the blog his opening and closing written arguments, as well as the judges publish the final decision.
- A news can be published in the blog showing a film or some pictures together with a description and the commenting of the trial and the final decision.

This is an amazing way of testing both the oral and the written skills needed for the exercise of all the legal professions. But this is also a tool to provide for the combination of "law in the books" with "law in action", giving the students an opportunity to mix deep study with great fun. Looking at it from the point of view of the students' assessment, in my view, it may even replace the final examination(s) (if allowed by the rules of the Faculty, as it is the case for my optional courses in Portugal).

This is a short example of some of the exercises I keep on doing for more than 30 years in the non-stop love story relationship with my students. Or to put it according to the title of this intervention, it is my way to sing again, and again, and again: «the rain in Spain stays mainly in the plane»....

*Eliza – The rain in Spain stays mainly in the plain.*
*Prof. Higgins – Again.*
*Eliza – The rain in Spain stays mainly in the plain.*

# Modern Teaching Methods in European Legal Education

*Francisco Balaguer Callejón*\*

## A. Introduction. A new approach after the health crisis

None of the participants in the Hannover Congress of December 2019 could even imagine that six months later a world as different as the one we are living in now was incubating. But this has been the case; the world was transformed in just two months since December 2019 to a point that we had never experienced. It was in Italy at the end of February 2020 that the dramatic extent of the change we are experiencing began to be seen in Europe. In my case I was able to experience it very directly because I had arrived in Milan on 16 February as a visiting professor at the University of Milan to teach a course that I finally had to give in part virtually due precisely to the closure of the university from 24 February. The same happened with the course I had planned to give at the beginning of March in Rouen, which I finally had to teach virtually.

My speech at the congress in Hannover focused precisely on my experience in online teaching since I had been teaching courses of this type for twelve years and I coordinate a master's that has been totally virtual for three years. It is precisely the pioneering nature of our master's at the University of Granada that has enabled it to continue to be taught with absolute normality despite the closure of the University of Granada during the health crisis. Naturally, when we designed the course, we did not imagine that we were going to face such a situation. The reasons for planning a virtual master's course were very different, but in these special circumstances, teaching online has been an enormous advantage that has allowed us to keep teaching without any change, as if nothing had happened around us.

But things certainly have happened. I myself have had to send videos to Milan and Rouen to be able to finish my teaching work virtually and the conference through Zoom that I had given from my mobile phone in a Berlin hotel in April 2019 for a Master in Brazil and which I indicated in my speech in Hannover as an example of the transformations we were experiencing already is now a common experience since the use of Zoom

---

\* Prof. Dr. Francisco Balaguer Callejón, University of Granada.

and other videoconferencing tools has become widespread throughout the world.

During these months I have seen how the universities where I teach have had to be radically reorganized, implementing massive virtual teaching techniques and making a great effort to keep up the academic activity. Naturally, the experience cannot be improvised so many things will surely have to be corrected in future in the activities that continue to be taught virtually. Online teaching has its specific characteristics and that is precisely one of the issues that were addressed in my presentation in Hannover and which are developed in this text.

Otherwise, the reflections I made in my presentation in Hannover are still fully valid after the outbreak of the health crisis. I would say that they have even been reinforced because the trends that we anticipated already back then will now be propelled as a consequence of the crisis. The world to come may be different from the one we knew, but not because it is going to mean a setback in globalization but because it is going to accelerate even more the transformations of the coordinates of space and time that had already appeared with the third globalization. All of the precautions that I pointed out in my presentation in Hannover and that are contained in this text must therefore be maintained and extended for the future.

It is very important, in any case, that we do not forget the fact that teaching in general but especially in the field of law must be a process of reflection. Perhaps reflection is not so necessary in order to learn a language or certain techniques in some disciplines, and it is possible to prioritize memory-based learning and practice. However, in the field of law this is not possible if we want to train jurists. Therefore, everything that contributes to reflection must be empowered to make comprehensive training possible, which is what the university must offer, bearing in mind that we not only train professionals[1] but must also contribute to forming individuals aware of the constitutional values that must inspire our life in society.

---

1 Cf. Smits, J. M., *European Legal Education, or: How to Prepare Students for Global Citizenship?*, The Law Teacher, Vol. 45 (2011), pp. 163–180.

*B. The position of legal studies in the context of globalization: The legitimacy of technology versus the legitimacy of the law*

The transformations in the relationship between technology and the law are an issue that we must consider prior to analysing the impact that technology may have on the development of new teaching methods in the legal field. This prior reflection is important because we are witnessing a decline in the legitimacy of the law (starting with the fundamental law, the national constitution itself) in favour of technology and the economy, the great legitimizing factors of the 21st century in the context of globalization.[2] To focus on only one basic idea about this relationship, I will say something that is well known: the modern world opened to a harmonious relationship between scientific development and constitutional law articulated around the notion of "law" and the constitution as a law. Both the scientific and legal laws that arise from parliament as an expression of the general will have been considered since the French Revolution to be an expression of one single rationality and the foundation of humanity's civilizational progress.

This harmonious, integrated relationship between technology and law was to continue for more than two hundred years in the history of modern constitutionalism until reaching the 21st century, when an increasingly intense tension between them appeared. Technological development in our time remains a legitimation factor associated with the idea of progress but which now faces legal and constitutional limits as an obstacle that may hinder the progress and the well-being that science brings to society. In particular, the technological companies that are leading the latest digital revolution offer continuous developments that appear before society as advances aimed at promoting consumers' welfare but which hide serious damages to fundamental rights for which they not only do not assume their responsibility but reject any control or sanctions, considering them to be an attack on the progress of humanity.[3]

This background is important in understanding the weakness with which legal studies permeate the cultural context that has established itself

---

2 Cf. Balaguer Callejón, F., *Constitution, démocratie et mondialisation. La légitimité de la Constitution face à la crise économique et aux réseaux sociaux*, in: *Mélanges en l'honneur du Professeur Dominique Rousseau. Constitution, justice, démocratie*. L.G.D.J, Paris 2020.

3 Cf. Balaguer Callejón, F., *Social network, società tecnologiche e democrazia*, in: *Nomos | Le attualità nel diritto*, n. 3, 2019: http://www.nomos-leattualitaneldiritto.it/wp-content/uploads/2020/02/Callejon-3-2019-ver.pdf [07.06.2020].

in recent years. It is a context in which, unlike other university disciplines, technology is not only an instrument that can serve to improve academic performance but also a competitor to the legal content we must teach. The new cultural patterns that are being developed through new technologies are also generating new paradigms that affect new generations of students' entire worldview, and that can also affect the way of understanding the legal system in general and the system of rights and freedoms it is inspired by in particular.[4]

There are many areas in which these transformations must be considered but I will give one very significant example: the possible use of algorithms for teaching.[5] There are already initiatives ("adaptive learning technologies") that propose using profiles developed by means of algorithms (which concern us very much from a legal point of view, for many reasons) to foster individualized learning by each student by selecting the teaching content and its scheduling.[6] Undoubtedly, this could increase productivity as in many other areas in which algorithms are used. However, these techniques involve developing psychological profiles that would be available to the technological companies that produce them, generating a potential risk factor as regards the rights of the student who submits to such "profiling". A deeply unlawful procedure would thus be used to learn law, if I may be allowed to express it so, taking into account the potential for injury to rights that it entails.

On the other hand, it is necessary to question ourselves as to whether this type of productivity can be an end in itself and if it can be considered a "teaching" methodology if we consider the value of teaching on the whole in building the student's personality. Reducing the concept of teaching to the assimilation of contents can be very useful from the point of view of effectiveness and productivity but very destructive if we consider that the university is not limited to offering material content in legal disciplines but it must also educate people, which means incorporating other

---

4 Cf. Balaguer Callejón, F., *Las dos grandes crisis del constitucionalismo frente a la globalización en el siglo XXI*, in: *Nomos | Le attualità nel diritto*, 2018: http://www.nomos-leattualitaneldiritto.it/wp-content/uploads/2018/09/Balaguer_Costituzionalismo.pdf [07.06.2020].

5 Cf. Jeong, A., *Quantitative Analysis of Interaction Patterns in Online Distance Education*, in: Zawacki-Richter, Olaf / Anderson, Terry, *Online Distance Education. Towards a Research Agenda*, AU Press, Athabasca University, Edmonton, 2014, pp. 403–420.

6 Cf. Pistone, M., *Law Schools and Technology: Where We Are and Where We Are Heading*, Villanova University School of Law Public Law and Legal Theory Working Paper (2015) No. 2015–1006.

content and open processes of reflection in all legal disciplines. The university should not become a production chain to train practical specialists, but should continue to be a centre for reflection to produce jurists with the ability to contribute to society not only with their technical knowledge of the rules, but also with a critical vision of the legal system. That is the way to make future advances in law possible in terms of its essential purpose of settle social conflicts and protecting fundamental rights.

## C. *Transformations in cultural patterns deriving from technology and their impact on the field of education*

Compared with the study methods of my generation, for example, university students today have great advantages but also great disadvantages.[7] Among the former, access to information is incomparably more agile, fast and comprehensive than a few decades ago. At the end of the seventies when I began to study at university, to know the legislation I had to wait for its official printed publication, which took several days to reach some places (hence the term of *vacatio legis* established for its entry into force). For judicial rulings it was even more difficult, because except for those coming from the Constitutional Court also published in the Official State Gazette, they only arrived through compilations of case-law and with a great delay. Scientific papers and books were often not available in university libraries and getting copies of them was sometimes impossible. In general, research followed the guidelines of previous centuries, except for photocopies, until the arrival of the first computers, in my case in 1984. On the other hand, the first electronic databases to which I had access were in 1985, though not in Spain but during my stay in the United States as a visiting professor at the IUPUI, in Indianapolis. In universities today, however, the problem is not access to information but selecting the information, given the large number of existing sources that make it virtually impossible to read everything affecting any subject of study, however limited it may be.

These advantages extend to the relationship with teachers: who could imagine in my time as a student that it would be possible to contact a professor directly at home to pose a question or clear up any doubt, especially on Sundays and holidays? However, this is perfectly possible today through

---

7 Cf. Balaguer Callejón, F., *La investigación en las Ciencias Jurídicas*, Revista general de derecho constitucional, Nº. 21 (2015).

email, as it is also possible to evaluate students' work in other parts of the world through videoconferences, or to give lessons directly from other countries via specific applications, even with a mobile phone.

In our online master's course, we have students of many nationalities and we communicate with them through the Internet, examining them via videoconferencing. And through my mobile telephone I was able to give a lecture last April from a hotel in Berlin, where I was staying for a congress, to a group of students from Teresina in Brazil. The bibliography that I give my students is always available on the Internet. It is open access and thanks to the Internet I can manage research papers at a distance and send papers or judicial decisions directly to the researchers. Not to mention word processors, which seem normal to us today but which I was only able to start using in 1984. My doctoral thesis, which I presented that same year, was written with a typewriter, making copies on tracing paper to avoid losing the text in the event of damage to the original document. Nowadays I have all the research papers in the cloud, with several copies stored in a pen drive, making it very difficult to lose these documents. On the other hand, the advantages we have as researchers also extend to the translation of scientific texts. The first texts I translated from German required the use of various types of dictionaries that have now been replaced by applications available on the Internet.

However, all these advantages have been accompanied by significant transformations in cultural patterns that affect universities, students and researchers alike. There are very specific matters that affect universities in particular, such as the ease of copying texts from the Internet, which entails very intense work of checking by teachers that was not previously seen as necessary. But there are others of a more general nature that lead university teaching to run into significant obstacles. This is the case of continuous dependence on social networks and mobile phones, encouraged by technological companies. This dependence creates a growing difficulty for students to concentrate and thus lower performance in classrooms, even if they are not allowed to use the mobile or the computer, as well as in preparing exams or papers. The average student of a few years ago had the text ahead and at most a music device to give them some company during the long study or work sessions. If they studied in the university library, they did not even have music, just the textbook.

The average student of today who is a digital native is subject to permanent stimuli that can interrupt their study session constantly either by WhatsApp messages, emails or continuous access to applications such as Facebook or Instagram, for example. This difficulty in concentrating is also evident in the classrooms, because even if they are not allowed to check their mobile phone, it is very common for them to do so secretly, using all kinds of strategies. This kind of student has other characteristics that imply a change in cultural patterns. For example, the vast majority (around 90 % in many European countries) are not informed about current affairs through the traditional media; on the contrary, they get fragmented, singled-out information through Internet applications[8] that send them information corresponding to their search or reading history, enclosing them in what Pariser[9] calls the "bubble filter". This kind of student is not accustomed to reading with continuity, but only occasionally and with content in short dosages of text. Most of their cultural experience is audio-visual, not written. Their access to information is increasingly sectorial and segmented, and their interest in fundamental rights or in law is usually weak. In the tension between technology and law, they have more stimuli in favour of technology than of law, because they continuously see advances that produce well-being and advantages, without awareness of the inconveniences linked to these advances. For example, they are not worried that their privacy or the secrecy of their communications is being violated, or that their personal data is being extracted from their activity on the Internet to build psychological profiles that can influence their purchasing habits or their political behaviour.

## D. *New teaching techniques in the field of law. Possibilities and limits*

Therefore, our starting point is a student who is not very motivated by legal contents and is more technology-oriented, even when that technology may violate their fundamental rights. The student has little training in legal matters and a general education that is increasingly fragmentary and less oriented towards writing in favour of audio-visual content offered through the Internet.[10] That means we necessarily have to adapt our teaching techniques to this new kind of student. The first question we must ask ourselves concerns designing the study material. The excellent manuals with which we studied, and the more modest ones we have written and

---

8   Cf. *The Cairncross Review. A sustainable future for journalism*, 12 February 2019, https://assets.publishing.service.gov.uk/government/uploads/system/uploads/attac hment_data/file/779882/021919_DCMS_Cairncross_Review_.pdf [07.06.2020].

9   Pariser, E., *The Filter Bubble. What the Internet Is Hiding from You*, Penguin Books (2011).

10  Cf. Colbran, S. / Gilding, A., *E-Learning in Australian Law Schools*, LegEdRev 10 (2013).

published ourselves, remain for the use of legal professionals. For students it is necessary to reduce the study material down to the structure of the courses taught, and to change the design of these study materials. I would say that, in general, the new manuals should follow the established guidelines for the preparation of teaching materials in online courses: a simpler, more uniform structure with sections that have minimum and maximum spread, with paragraphs that are also limited in terms of the number of lines they should contain, underlining or highlighting the main ideas, etc.

The second problem is that of the practical approach. Today's students do not want, and possibly do not need, great insights into the world or law. They live in a reality full of immediate urgencies and in which it is necessary to sacrifice to some extent the conceptual systems that served us to understand the reality of our time. This practical aspect implies a different orientation for the teaching material and also for the way of teaching it, less focused on the master class and passive transmission of knowledge. An active way of teaching is therefore necessary in which student participation allows us to open up the path of knowledge together.

Taking into account all of these transformations, the limits should also be considered, especially the limits to the use of new technologies. The question is, should we turn the class into a show to facilitate learning? Is it necessary to incorporate social networks in education, for example, through Facebook, Instagram or Twitter to motivate students?

Personally, I have a very critical approach to social networks for many reasons that I cannot explain in detail here and I have serious doubts that they can contribute to the construction of a serious, thoughtful debate on the legal issues that interest us in any minimal depth. I believe that the cultural patterns promoted by technological companies do not contribute to a truly participatory communicative process that is respectful of people's rights and positive for democratic processes. Therefore, I do not consider social networks to be among the technological innovations we should consider in organizing new teaching methods in legal matters. All of this is said with no detriment to my respect for other opinions and other practices in this regard.

## E. *E-learning teaching in legal studies*

E-learning is a technique or to be more precise a set of techniques that can be useful to organize distance education and also to incorporate some of its aspects into classroom teaching. The combination of part of the methodology of online teaching and traditional education, integrating both online teaching and face-to-face teaching, is a positive experience or, at least it has been in my case. Personally, I have been teaching online courses for 12 years (I started in 2007) in the context of two Jean Monnet Chairs I have held and for three years now in an online master's that I co-ordinate. The courses, at a rate of two per year with a total of 12 credits, were blended whereas the master's in which I teach a total of 10 annual credits, is completely online.

The study method for a virtual course is different from a classroom one. Studying through virtual teaching methods is more autonomous, so it requires responsible time management to meet the course objectives the teacher has planned. Likewise, it is essential to adopt a participatory attitude, so that the teacher's guidelines can be seen as stimuli to help handle the available resources properly, especially through the Internet, and in searching for information sources related to the topics proposed to carry out activities and for the joint debate to be carried out via the platform.

The course materials should be designed and the studies scheduled from the perspective of continuous interaction between theory and practice. Thus, reading the materials is not a mere theoretical experience but serves as the basis for reflection and to carry out the subsequent activities through the forums or the papers created by the students. It is in these activities where the knowledge previously acquired by reading the materials can be applied and the students can develop and express their own opinions regarding the issues that are the subject of the course.

Virtual teaching tools include access to the syllabus, forums, internal mail, and specific questionnaires on self-control over learning and also recorded master classes or videoconferences to discuss the topics on the course with the students. They must be used according to a very detailed teaching schedule established in the calendar and in the time allotted for each course. The use of available techniques should make it possible for the participants to be able to say that at the end of the course that they have truly learned and that they have greater motivation to reflect in the future on the issues of the course. In legal matters, it is not simply about assimilating knowledge, but about developing a critical attitude as regards the topics in the course.

Evaluation in virtual education must be carried out through specific procedures, taking into account that the platform itself carries out detailed monitoring of each student's activity. Evaluation is based on implementation of virtual teaching activities: access to the contents of the materials via the platform, active participation in the forums and carrying out work on the topics previously established by the teacher. In any case, it is important to establish the means of checking on the identity of the students, such as videoconferences in which they present the work and discuss it with the teacher, giving adequate responses to the observations, comments and questions made regarding the work and the course materials.

Virtual education is not geared towards the mere diffusion of knowledge but towards promoting personal reflection among those taking part in the courses about the specific topics addressed in them. This capacity for personal reflection is what should be most valued both in participation in the forums and in the presentation of the work. In any case, a prior condition for a positive assessment must be knowledge of the syllabus of the course available on the platform, so that both the intervention in the forums and the preparation of the work must be based on that prior knowledge.

## F. *The experience of the health crisis*

As long as the health alert situation continues, it will be impossible to resume face-to-face teaching. However, everything will pass and surely by the next academic year we will be teaching the usual classes. The experience accumulated in these months for those who had not previously taught virtual education will surely be very positive. However, it was inevitable that without prior training in virtual teaching, what has been done so far is simply offering virtual classroom teaching, which is very different from virtual teaching. Therefore, it will be necessary to continue training teachers and students in virtual teaching techniques for it to be given effectively.

Again, it must be emphasized that teaching is a reflective process and that this not only cannot be lost but also must be enhanced with techniques of online teaching for courses and masters. Naturally, virtual teaching platforms also offer the possibility of accumulating knowledge and contrasting what has been learned through test-type questionnaires that can be used by students as a means of monitoring their own learning. But it is important in the field of education in law that we do not forget the need to foster students' ability to reflect so that they not only get to know the legal field but above all so that they may become jurists. Our ambition cannot be simply to train legal professionals, but also to forming good jurists.

In my case, taking advantage of the time available during the quarantine since I did not have to travel and thus saved a lot of time, I prepared additional material for my students in Milan and Rouen through a cartoon book that metaphorically poses some of the problems that constitutional law has to face at this time, and especially with the health crisis. It is not a book with which they are going to learn or memorize content, but it can encourage their ability to reflect on the great problems of our time through the metaphors it contains in each vignette.

The use of metaphors to explain legal problems is very positive. I have to say that I learned it from Vasco Pereira da Silva, who I imitated in the title of my work on "El Tratado de Lisboa en el diván", which after being published in the *Revista Española de Derecho Constitucional* in Spain was also published in Italy under the title "Il Trattato di Lisbona sul lettino dell'analista" in *Quaderni della Rassegna di Diritto Pubblico Europeo*, and in Brazil, under the title "O Tratado de Lisboa no divã", in the *Revista Brasileira de Estudos Constitucionais*. As I indicated in those publications, the title was not mine: "strange as the title of this work may seem, it is not the first to place a text or a legal institution on the psychoanalyst's couch. My good friend Vasco Pereira da Silva already submitted the contentious-administrative Portuguese to the divan test in an excellent book (Edições Almedina, Coimbra, 2005). Its application to the Lisbon Treaty was inevitable, given the tormented image of Europe that the Treaty projects".

We have to remember Lichtenberg's sentence: the metaphor is much more intelligent than its author (*"Die Metapher ist weit klüger als ihre Verfasser"*), which indicates that the metaphor has many more interpretations than we suggest and that it opens up an infinity of reflective processes. All those who read this text and were present at my speech in Hannover will remember the frog metaphor with which I always try to explain the deterioration of our system of fundamental rights confronted with social networks and technological companies. As it is not as radical and brutal as a *coup d'état*, which was the previous known form of massive damage to constitutional rights, and as they offer us many positive things, like the frog we feel pleasant warmth as the water heats up. Those positive things that technological companies bring to our lives disarm our ability to critically reflect on the dark side, the effects on privacy, the right to protection of personal data, the secrecy of communications, etc. If it had been a *coup d'état*, like throwing the frog into a container of boiling water, then just like the frog we would have jumped out and saved ourselves. At the moment, not everything is lost, but the water's temperature is continuing to rise and our comfort still outweighs the disadvantages. Will it always be like this or will we have to regret one day not having jumped out, not having demanded that technological companies respect our fundamental rights?

From the perspective of the science of law, which we must serve, Peter Häberle[11] reminds us that in the classic texts of W. v. Humboldt science is characterized as a permanent search for truth. The German constitutionalist has reformulated that reference of W. v. Humboldt specifically for legal science: "the science of Law is the permanent search for Justice because Justice is the Truth of Law".[12] This idea of justice as the truth of law implies a specific commitment for the jurist, in the awareness that their work is not merely descriptive but implies a transformational purpose because it is ordered to search and achieve justice.

In this role that corresponds to us as jurists, critical capacity must be realistic because, as Helmuth Schulze-Fielitz says, "it is a specific and critical task of science to mention and anticipate problems. In this, it differs from politics, which aims above all to provide legitimacy".[13] At the same time, it is essential that we also offer a positive message, because criticism cannot limit itself to stating the problems but also to offering proposals for solutions that enable them to be solved. We do not know the world that awaits us after the pandemic, but we do know that the ability to understand and transform it is in our hands, to make it possible to implement constitutional rights. Legal Teaching methods and techniques must be oriented to achieving this goal.

---

11  See in the following Häberle, P., *Un Jurista universal nacido en Europa. Entrevista a Peter Häberle, por Francisco Balaguer Callejón*, ReDCE, núm. 13, Enero-Junio (2010): https://www.ugr.es/~redce/REDCE13/articulos/12Entrevista.htm [07.06.2020].

12  Ibid.

13  Schulze-Fielitz, H., *El lado oscuro de la Ley Fundamental*, ReDCE, Número 12, julio-diciembre (2009): https://www.ugr.es/~redce/REDCE12/articulos/09Schulze _Fielitz.htm [07.06.2020].

## G. *Conclusions*

As we have seen, we are experiencing transcendental social changes that are going to be greatly amplified with the health crisis and which are inevitably affecting the way law is taught in our universities. Some of these changes imply new cultural patterns and new paradigms in the relationship between technology and law, which generate additional difficulties for teaching law to those that may exist in other university disciplines. It is very important in these processes of redefining work and teaching methods that we never forget the principles on which all democratic and constitutional legal systems are based, in particular the reaffirmation of fundamental rights in the contents and in the teaching process and the rejection of any model that is based exclusively on efficiency and productivity without taking into account the dignity of students and teachers.

# A more European Legal Education – Lessons to be Learned

*Andreas Schwartze*[*]

## A. Introduction

Since more than 20 years there are different attempts and ideas in Europe to create a legal education that is not in the traditional way mainly directed to national rule systems[1] but opens up to the European Union – or the internal market – as a whole. This development has been accelerated by the declaration of Bologna in 1999,[2] which sets a common structure to all academic studies with the degrees of a Bachelor, a Master and a Doctor. Although at first glance the Bologna process is related only to the form of studies, the content of legal education is affected as well. In the following years it was discussed how and to what extent especially European Union law could be integrated into the curricula of law faculties. In recent times the European Law Faculties Association (ELFA), joined by the European Law Institute (ELI), has initiated a working group concerning the model of a "European Jurist" as a goal for the future.[3]

The skills of this new role model are as follows:[4] The European Jurist should be able to act as an international manager of legal services. He should speak more than one, better three languages[5] and should study abroad (at least one year) to understand foreign legal systems. He should

---

[*] Prof. Dr. Andreas Schwartze, LL.M. (EUI), University of Innsbruck.

1 Still in many European countries legal education seems to be very nationalistic, particularly in France and Southern countries, see Fauvarque-Cosson, *The Rise of Comparative law: a Challenge for Legal Eduction in Europe*, Seventh Walter van Gerven Lecture, 2007, 11.

2 https://www.eurashe.eu/library/bologna_1999_bologna-declaration-pdf/ [20.05.2020].

3 The first meeting took place in 2018, https://elfa-edu.org/elfa_elimeeting/ [20.05.2020].

4 See Martinek, *Juristenausbildung für Europa*, in: Bergmans (ed.), *Jahrbuch der Rechtsdidaktik 2013/2014*, 11 (27 et seqq).

5 English as the most widespread second language is a must, see Jamin / van Caenegem, *The Internationalisation of Legal Education: General Report*, in: Jamin / van Caenegem (eds), *The Internationalisation of Legal Education*, 2016, 3 (25), French and/or German would cover other very important languages in Europe, but as a

be trained in finding legal solutions of common problems and introduced to the main essentials of the different legal systems per se, instead of being treated in positivistic details and doctrinal intricacies of a national legal order. The European Jurist should be familiar with different legal systems in the Member States of the Union and should understand similarities, differences and specialities of foreign legal systems, added with historic roots of norms and comparative jurisprudence.

Therefore, it is necessary to amend the curricula of law faculties and law schools throughout the EU. Because the situation is more or less the same everywhere all over Europe it makes sense to think about at least a common structure and common general principles of legal education in all Member States of the Union and beyond that throughout the continent. At the annual conference in Torino 2019 ELFA has adopted a correspondent resolution:

"universities and public institutions should facilitate the development of common curricula between law schools of different countries as a means to positively contribute to the preparation of European legal professionals".[6]

First, I will shortly describe why a more European legal education is necessary (B). Then the focus will be on the question of what things need to be taught to qualify as a European Jurist[7] (C). In the following part I am trying to compare curricula from selected law faculties of three legal systems, which are closely related, because they are members of the same (German or Middle-European) legal family (D). Finally, I would like to show some aspects of legal education, which could be harmonized or unified Europe-wide to amend them in the direction of a more European legal education (E).

---

third one or in addition one of the smaller languages also has its benefits. Storme, *The consequences of European unification for legal education in the member states*, European Review 2001, 135 (143), is in favour of languages that are spoken in more than one European country, besides the language mentioned (German, French, English) also Dutch and Swedish.

6  ELFA Resolution April 11/12 2019 (Torino, IT).

7  On the question of how law should be taught see *Pereira da Silva*, "My Fair Lady": Introductive Lecture, in this volume.

## B. Reasons for a more European legal education

The main argument in favour of a truly European legal education is that undoubtedly the relevant legal norms are increasingly originating from other than national sources. The European Union, as well as other international organizations, is more and more determining the national legal systems of its Member States by issuing binding instruments like regulations and directives. Beyond that, numerous non-binding rules ("soft law") created by transnational initiatives (so-called "formulating agencies") are influencing the behaviour of people, for instance contract parties,[8] in different European States. Even in areas that earlier seemed to be unaffected by the "Europeanization" of law, like divorces, bankruptcies or criminal proceedings,[9] at least unified EU-rules in Private International Law and International Procedure have been enacted.[10] That means that the practice of advocates, judges, administrators and business lawyers is less and less determined by purely national regulations but instead contains more and more international elements, although with different importance. Therefore, more European respective international content should be integrated into the legal education in all European nations.

## C. The subjects to be taught

Of course, it is necessary in every legal education to introduce the students to the main areas of law, as there are on the one side the national private and public law and on the other side international law and the law of the European Union. Hence, courses concerning each of these subjects are regularly a part of recent law school curricula in Europe. In my opinion more European legal studies should not so much focus on such a separation between national and international/EU law but integrate the European and international elements into most of the courses on national law, because that is what a lawyer working in Europe needs more and more.

---

8  For example UNIDROIT with the Principles of International Commercial Contracts (PICC), or the ICC with the INCOTERMS.

9  Compare Storme, *The consequences of European unification for legal education in the member states,* European Review 2001, 135 (138).

10  Regarding the teaching of Private International Law see Kadner-Graziano, *Private International Law in Legal Education in Europe and Selected other countries,* in: von Hein/Kieninger/Rühl (eds), *How European is European Private International Law,* 2019, 333.

Against that idea some authors argue in favour of a de-nationalized legal education, for instance to teach European tort law instead of Austrian, French or Swedish tort law. From my point of view this is currently not possible, because the European and international systems of rules are still fragmented and often pointillistic, compared to the national bodies of legal norms, which have been elaborated over a very long time, and grown to nearly complete and mainly consistent legal regimes.

In addition, to combine the teaching of national law provisions with the instruction on European and international legal norms, most of the subjects on domestic regulations should be enriched with comparative law aspects,[11] especially from neighbouring legal systems (for instance in Austria with aspects of German law[12] and Swiss law). Usually, legal education starts with the internal legal system, e.g. in Austria with Austrian law, in Germany with German law. Mostly foreign law or comparative law is taught later, often as a free-standing course,[13] giving an overview on the comparative method and an introduction into some foreign legal systems, in the last year of the basic legal education or even within a supplementary study (often for an extra degree like an LL.M.) abroad. This is motivated by the fear that students, who are exposed to other legal systems too early – that is, before they have learned well enough one coherent set of rules, their domestic one –, will get confused by the information about different and conflicting regulations.

However, from my perspective, it seems to be too late to shift information on foreign legal systems to the last semester: Then students to a greater or lesser extent are locked-in within the one and only legal order they have explored for a long time throughout their whole studies. Hence, they are less open and motivated to learn about different legal views and various legal solutions to given problems.[14] Therefore, it would be better

---

11 More cautious Bitas, *"Comparative Law" and the 21st Century Legal Practice*, 24 SAcLJ (2012), 319 (326, 336). On the relevance of comparative law in legal education Demleitner, *Comparative Law in Legal Education*, in: Reimann/Zimmermann (eds), *Oxford Handbook of Comparative Law*, 2nd ed, 2019, 320; see Schwartze, § 4: *Comparative Law*, in: Riesenhuber (ed.), *European Legal Methodology*, 2017, 61 (83 et seq.).

12 For connections in the area of civil law compare Schwartze, *Das ABGB und das deutsche Zivilrecht*, in: Barta et al. (ed.), *Kontinuität im Wandel – 200 Jahre ABGB (1811 – 2011)*, 2012, 201.

13 In favour of such type of courses Bitas, *"Comparative Law" and the 21st Century Legal Practice*, 24 SAcLJ (2012), 319 (336 et seq.).

14 See Husa, *Comparative law in legal education – building a legal mind for a transnational world*, The Law Teacher 2018, 201 (211).

to start integration of comparative aspects already at the beginning of their studies.[15] That does not mean to overload lectures for beginners with comparative aspects, since the share of foreign law could be increased from semester to semester. Towards the end of the studies there could be even obligatory courses on maybe two or three foreign legal systems, ideally chosen by the students out of several options offered.

## D. Comparing three national models

To analyse the structure and general aspects of law school curricula I have chosen three of them, stemming from Austria (Innsbruck, the faculty where I am teaching), Germany (Hannover, the faculty I have been educated) and Switzerland (Bern, a closely connected faculty).

At the University of Innsbruck in the traditional diploma study of law[16] we start with an introductory phase of one year, mainly filled with Criminal Law, Roman Private Law and History of Law. Then the main studies follow, where within two years all aspects of Private Law and Public Law are taught in detail. The last year is devoted to a specialization as preferred by the student, with the option between different "baskets" of elective courses ("fields of concentration"), one out of seven combines transnational subjects under the title "Foreign Law and Law Comparison". Until that very last part of the studies there are three courses on international aspects: Private International Law (combined with Civil Law) and lectures on EU law and public international law.

In Hannover at the Leibniz University the study of law with orientation to the state examination[17] is divided into two parts, each two years long. In the first part the three main areas of law are offered: Private Law, Public Law and Criminal Law, complemented by some subsidiary subjects. During this part only one international course, EU law, is taught. The second part is for specialization or "focus studies" and the preparation for the state exam.

---

15 Husa, *Comparative law in legal education – building a legal mind for a transnational world*, The Law Teacher 2018, 201 (204).
16 Universität Innsbruck, *Diplomstudium Rechtswissenschaften*, https://www.uibk.ac.at /studium/angebot/d-rechtswissenschaften/index.html.de [30.03.2020].
17 Leibniz Universität Hannover, *Rechtswissenschaften (Staatsexamen)*, https://www.u ni-hannover.de/de/studium/studienangebot/info/studiengang/detail/rechtswissens chaften/ [30.03.2020].

At the University of Bern the study of law is organized following the Bachelor/Master model. The Bachelor course[18] starts with one year of introductory studies, although the students are directly thrown into the general parts (one third) of Private, Public and Criminal Law. This is followed by the main studies during two years, with the rest (two thirds) of Private, Public and Criminal Law and the entire Business Law. Included are some basic subjects (Roman Law, Legal History, Legal Theory, Legal Philosophy, Legal Sociology) and two international courses, one on EU law (in Switzerland!) and the other an introduction to international public law. This three-year Bachelor program is followed by a Master program[19] of one and a half year, offering a very wide range of 14 to 16 optional subjects which could be combined to five core studies, where one of it is "International and European law".

### E. Common principles of a more European legal education

Even this rough comparison of these curricula regarding the education in three strongly related legal systems shows significant differences.

The duration of legal education is 4 years in Austria and Germany, but 4,5 years in Switzerland – and within the EU there are even countries where 5 years are necessary (like in Belgium or like the diploma studies of Italian law in Innsbruck) and others, where 3 or 3,5 years are sufficient.[20] There is a trend to require 5 years, which would be in line with the Bologna declaration, usually asking for a 3 years / 2 years structure (like the Business law studies in Innsbruck, which follow the Bachelor/Master format), but even a 4 years / 1 year model would be possible. As the Bologna declaration stated, it is of course questionable if a Bachelor degree after 3 years is enough for an "appropriate level of education" for legal professions like advocates or judges. Anyway, these time frames are ideal conceptions and many students need at least one or two additional semesters, especially if they spend one or two semesters abroad, which is highly recommended.

---

18  Universität Bern, *Rechtswissenschaftliche Fakultät – Bachelor Rechtswissenschaften*, https://www.rechtswissenschaft.unibe.ch/studium/studienprogramme/bachelor_r echtswissenschaft/index_ger.html [30.03.2020].

19  Universität Bern, *Rechtswissenschaftliche Fakultät – Master Rechtswissenschaften*, https://www.rechtswissenschaft.unibe.ch/studium/studienprogramme/master_rec htwissenschaft/index_ger.html [30.03.2020].

20  Storme, *The consequences of European unification for legal education in the member states*, European Review 2001, 135 (141).

Only Austria and Switzerland start with an introduction of one year. However, the Austrian system alone offers a basis in legal history, especially with the mandatory course on Roman law (in Switzerland this is part of the main studies, in Germany it is only an optional subject), and it concentrates this phase of the studies on Criminal law (this will be changed soon in Innsbruck, because the introductory studies will be reduced to only one semester and Criminal law will move into the main part of the studies). In Bern Criminal Law is taught only in part next to the other two main subjects. I think an introduction into law and the legal studies is necessary, preferably lasting one year, and it should encompass basic subjects like legal history (as in Innsbruck), legal philosophy and legal sociology, and moreover an overview on international aspects of law including the comparative method.

Most of the European and international subjects in all three educational systems that were presented above, are shifted to the last part of the studies, when students take optional special courses. EU law alone, but merely as an overview, is part of the main studies in all three curricula, next to international public law, again not in detail, which is obligatory in Bern and Innsbruck, and Private International Law as a mandatory subject just in Austria.[21]

The intensity of studies in international law should be enhanced by declaring all three transnational subjects (EU law, international public law and Private International Law) mandatory and by raising the weekly hours of teaching. In addition, EU-specific and comparative aspects should be integrated into the teaching of all main areas of law, whether it is Private, Public, Criminal or Business law. Because the overall workload for students should not be raised, the teaching of the national legal system must be reduced correspondingly. This could be done mainly by concentrating on its essentials like structure, methods and guiding principles,[22] and leaving out the details, which could later rather easy be looked up if necessary.

These are my proposals for the general legal education of all students. From my perspective, it would be wrong to divide the training of jurists,

---

21 This is in line with a survey on the education in international fields of law in Germany, Austria and Switzerland, see Hobe / Marauhn, *Lehre des internationalen Rechts im deutschsprachigen Raum – Herausforderungen und Entwicklungspotentiale*, in: Hobe / Marauhn (eds), *Lehre des internationalen Rechts – zeitgemäß?*, 2017, 11.

22 Husa, *Comparative law in legal education – building a legal mind for a transnational world*, The Law Teacher 2018, 201 (209).

like some colleagues prefer,[23] into one type limited to the national legal system and another type for European and international affairs.

---

23 *E.g.* Heringa, *European Legal Education or Legal Education in Europe*, MJ 2011, 221 (224).

# Is there an Optimal (and also Modern) Learning Method of Law in the Context of Educating International Lawyers?

*Dimitrios Parashu*[*]

I feel extremely honored and pleased to participate in this Conference, which gives me the opportunity to share with you some of my own experiences regarding the teaching of law. The present panel, due to its personal composition, is at the very core of the necessity of using modern teaching methods and their best possible reception.

Having in mind the numerous law lessons which I had the honor to follow as a student, and also the several ones which I had the honor to deliver so far to the next generation of legal professionals, I get to a primary conclusion: There seems to be no universal scheme for an optimal learning method of law, since everybody has their own relevant likes and dislikes.[1] Given my Greek roots of course, I have always sought for teaching in a

---

[*] Dr. iur. Dimitrios Parashu, MLE, Dikigoros (Greek Lawyer), Habilitand and Research Associate at the Faculty of Law, Gottfried Wilhelm Leibniz University of Hanover.

[1] Conf. Meyer-Kretschmer, C., *Lernmethoden Jura* (April 7th, 2019), retrieved at http://www.juraindividuell.de/blog/lernmethoden-jura/ [last accessed on 06.05.2020]; Charles, G.-U., *Defining What's Socratic* (NY Times, February 22nd, 2013), retrieved at https://www.nytimes.com/roomfordebate/2011/12/15/rethinking-how-the-law-is-taught/defining-whats-socratic [last accessed on 06.05.2020]; Pustilnik, A. C., *The Socratic Method Keeps the Student Thinking* (NY Times, December 16th, 2011), retrieved at https://www.nytimes.com/roomfordebate/2011/12/15/rethinking-how-th e-law-is-taught/the-socratice-method-keeps-the-student-thinking [last accessed on 06.05.2020]; West, R., *'Socratic' Teaching is a Thing of the Past* (NY Times, December 15th, 2011), retrieved at https://www.nytimes.com/roomfordebate/2011/12/15/rethi nking-how-the-law-is-taught/socratic-teaching-is-a-thing-of-the-past [last accessed on 06.05.2020); Wilkins, D. B., *Keep the Socratic Teaching Method, But Change the Focus* (NY Times, December 15th, 2011), retrieved at https://www.nytimes.com/roomford ebate/2011/12/15/rethinking-how-the-law-is-taught/keep-the-socratic-teaching-meth od-but-change-the-focus [last accessed on 06.05.2020]; Dinerstein, R. D., *There Are Limitations to the Socratic Method* (NY Times, December 15th, 2011), retrieved at https://www.nytimes.com/roomfordebate/2011/12/15/rethinking-how-the-law-is-ta ught/there-are-limitations-to-the-socratic-method [last accessed on 06.05.2020].

mere (but always modern) Socratic[2] way, using certain μαιευτική elements – and thereby trying to reach scientific truth through successive questions towards lecture participants.

I feel extremely honored and glad to have had the opportunity to follow the brilliant guest lectures delivered by our dear Professor Hugg over the last week here in Hanover; as he described his own vision, in a quite laconic way, it is important for us as lecturers to understand that "we want the best for our students". Thus meaning, we as lecturers should do everything humanly possible to ease and support both their active participation and an efficient information reception within academic lessons of law.

One of the most important differentiations of learning methods is the choice of the channel over which an information reaches the mind:[3] The auditory channel uses the ear as an entry gate, while the visual one uses the eye and both not only use different entrance gates, but also address different brain regions.[4] This is of importance even vis-à-vis the undisputed fact that in contemporary legal education, quite usually a traditional whole-class teaching method is still used,[5] "in which the lecturer stands at the blackboard, teaches the whole class the established body of knowledge, tests the (students) with questions and ensures a disciplined class environment".[6]

These elements of subjective channels of learning despite traditional approaches gain even more importance in the context of educating international lawyers. Having the honor to serve within the well-known ELPIS program, my conclusion is that the complexity of respective legal orders can only be further understood by using methods of Comparative Law (namely in a micro or macro way of comparison) and varying languages, in order to try out acquired theoretical knowledge especially in cross-border cases of legal importance.

My own experience shows that, regardless the extent of using modern teaching methods, not only the law itself, but merely psychology proves to

---

2  Conf. Charles (op.cit.); Pustilnik (op.cit.); West (op.cit.); Wilkins (op.cit.); Dinerstein (op.cit.).
3  Conf. Meyer-Kretschmer (op.cit.).
4  Conf. ibid.
5  Conf. Reville, W., *The Reason Why Modern Teaching Methods Don't Work* (March 2nd, 2015), "Irish Times", https://www.irishtimes.com/news/science/the-reason-why -modern-teaching-methods-don-t-work-1.2115219; last accessed on 06.05.2020].
6  See Reville (op.cit.).

be of the utmost importance.[7] To be more concrete, a mere obstacle in participating actively in academic legal lectures, especially for students of an international program like ELPIS, is quite always the element of fear; *i.e.* mainly the fear of asking or answering questions, be it because of linguistic difficulties, be it because of a student's "shy" personal disposition. But – as Fassbinder would have put it through his brilliant movie of 1974 – "Angst essen Seele auf", meaning that fear of any kind could possible eat up one's soul.

We have the special honor and pleasure to host today some of our most distinguished and brilliant master students, who have already shown in the lecture room that they are practically "fearless" in front of achieving a scientific truth. It is now time to give them the floor!

---

7 Conf. Parameswaran, K., *The Psychology of Legal Pedagogy: Introducing Interface between Law and Psychology*, in: International Journal of Indian Psychology, Vol. 3, Issue 1 (Oct.-Dec. 2015), pp. 158 et seqq. (to be seen also at http://oaji.net/articles/2 015/1170-1443955822.pdf).

# Wording the Needs of Innovative Teaching in Law

*Kersi Kurti*<sup></sup>

## A. *Introduction*

Learning is an organized process, designed to achieve the acquisition of knowledge in certain areas. Learning methods are the ways and procedures students and teachers use during and outside the lecture. Sometimes it is difficult to think about changing the teaching methodology, especially when this approach has been successful in the past.

However, more than seventy years of research around the world have enabled us to come to certain conclusions on teaching and learning, which can be shown to be useful for legal education.[1] Historically the methods have evolved, changed, refined and modernized in accordance with social, economic and political developments. Time changes so innovation is a necessity. Innovations happen all around us, every day. Teaching methods need innovation. Teaching method is accelerating transformation with the development of science and technology progress. Every teacher has her or his own style of teaching. Although it is not the teacher's job to entertain students, it is vital to engage them in the learning process.

The ways teachers try to explain lessons are varied and numerous. Making the lesson as interesting as possible is important because in this way the lessons will be not monotonous and consequently students don't lose the interest in learning new knowledge. In education, innovation means doing what's best for all students. Teacher-student interaction can be seen as exchange, as collaboration and as an intellectual confrontation.

The biggest challenge for any teacher is capturing each student's attention, and conveying ideas effectively enough to create a lasting impression. Innovative methods can provide law students significant experience with practice and opportunities to deal with issues of legal profession. With new technologies that provide instant access to information, the mechani-

---

* Kersi Kurti is an LL.M. Student (European Legal Practice Joint Degree, Hanover/ Lisbon), currently in her 3rd semester.
1 See Treuthart, Mary Pat, *Teknikat e mësimit interaktiv* (Interactive lesson techniques), Gonzaga 2007, p. 1.

cal memorization of doctrines is no longer as essential as it used to be. By helping students develop various skills such as: critical thinking, legal analysis, creative problem solving, effective oral communication, legal writing, negotiation and advocacy, they will be given better opportunities to be so successful members in this new legal environment.[2]

### B. *The aid of innovative methods*

Innovation does not necessarily mean to always create something from nothing.[3] Comparable to any given good science project, it is pretty much based on researching pre-existing solutions in order to come up with a new hypothesis.[4] Innovations include various aspects of education provision. These innovations stimulate changes in the provision and management of higher education and, thus, challenge the 'traditional' model of university and its future. Change is difficult everywhere because people are resistant to change. As Lloyd Armstrong writes, "Individuals generally are wary of changes that challenge old assumptions and require new skills to succeed."[5]

There are many of smart and creative people in colleges and universities. Developing a veritable culture of innovation requires actually the use of comparable intelligence and relevant creativity.[6] In order for innovation to take place, there must obviously be a perceived need for change, and therefore an inspiration – including the strong belief that there is a problem to solve – must be the first step in a process at the brink of innovation.[7]

With the aid of innovative methods the deadlocks will break down and impasses that might occur during our learning process can be avoided. Innovation is important to the advancement of society. Innovation in education mean, not only teachers but students as well need to use all their possibility to find something new. So they need to look at problems not as be-

---

2  See ibid.
3  Conf. Northwest Missouri State University, *Why Innovation Absolutely Matters in Education* (January 08, 2018), https://online.nwmissouri.edu/articles/education/inn ovation-matters-in-education.aspx [01.06.2020].
4  Conf. ibid.
5  Armstrong, Lloyd, *Barriers to Innovation and Change in Higher Education*, TIAA-CREF Institute (www.tiaa-crefinstitute.org) [01.06.2020].
6  Conf. Swanger, Dustin, *Innovation in Higher Education: Can Colleges Really Change?* June 2016 (https://www.fmcc.edu/about/files/2016/06/Innovation-in-Higher-Educat ion.pdf [01.06.2020]), p. 47.
7  Conf. ibid, p. 25.

fore and as a result to solve them in a different way. Innovation develops education, because through it students are able to use their intelligence more to solve problems.

By combining a variety of disciplines to come to a different conclusion, innovation does not simply teach ABC and 123, but goes beyond the basics. To be familiar with basic knowledge is obviously essential because students make a lot of researches in order to be able to find solutions and the best possible answers.[8] The poet William Butler Yeats once said: "Education should not be the filling of a pail, but the lighting of a fire."[9] From this we understand the importance of the role of innovation in education.


## C. Innovation in education

Innovation in education means finding any way a teacher can in order to reach all of their students.[10] All the relevant factors, meaning teachers, their lesson form and the curriculum structure have to be flexible.[11] Teachers have to get their students moreover to think and, following that, to ask questions.[12] They need to enhance their curiosity and accordingly to find every possible way to keep the students interested.[13] This means being willing and flexible to adjust to what exactly and how exactly is taught.[14] Teachers need to keep students constantly engaged and, at the same time, excited in order to learn. They have to create a room of safety for them within the classroom, in order to be allowed to make mistakes, to take risks, and accordingly to ask questions.[15]

Independence and cooperation, practice and applicability, variety and comprehensiveness, exploration and creation are some aspects where innovation should be strengthened. Theories, principles, their practices and ap-

---

8 Conf. Northwest Missouri State University, *Why Innovation Absolutely Matters in Education* (January 08, 2018), https://online.nwmissouri.edu/articles/education/innovation-matters-in-education.aspx [01.06.2020].

9 Norfolk, Sherry / Stenson, Jane (ed.), *Engaging Community Through Storytelling: Library and Community Programming*, Santa Barbara/Denver 2017, p. 89.

10 Conf. The SHARE Team, *Innovation in Education: What Does It Mean, and What Does It Look Like?*, March, 2018, https://resilienteducator.com/classroom-resources/educational-innovations-roundup/ [01.06.2020].

11 Conf. ibid.

12 Conf. ibid.

13 Conf. ibid.

14 Conf. ibid.

15 Conf. ibid.

plications have always helped to learn the law. Between the several legal theories and their accurate and realistic application is always a connection.[16] But the subject in hand has not been viewed regularly with its corresponding social, economic and also political connections.[17] "Law as it is invariably known consists of multifarious areas such as Corporate Law, Intellectual Property Law, Criminal Law, Family Law and Environmental Law etc. each linked with the other"[18], and therefore "the task relevant for teaching these subjects is to bridge the gap existing between them."[19] Relating and demonstrating through real-life situations will make the material easy to understand and easy to learn.

A good suggestion is for the learning environment to engage teachers and students. Active learning requires students to share responsibility for acquiring knowledge, skills, and values. Among the many dimensions of active learning are writing, discussion, peer teaching, research, internships, and community experiences. These kinds of active experiences help students understand and integrate new information.

Asking helpful questions is one of the most important techniques a teacher can develop. Questions can engage students in the process of understanding. I think that asking questions helps us, the students, to build our basic understanding. Answers to asking questions should form the basis of basic understanding on which other types of questions can then be built to foster greater understanding and application. Such questions also help clarify the meaning of words or phrases and help analyze details of the sequence of events for greater comprehension. A good discussion can help us as students to learn the importance of seeking answers to important questions and the value of listening and learning from the comments, ideas, and experiences of others. It can also help us maintain a level of concentration and participation in the auditor.

It is better for us when teacher are motivators and communication partners. We as student want teacher's advices on the activities that we will develop and we want that teachers accept the students' feedback on the method to be developed. Teacher should create the opportunity for the students to be free to ask questions. Personally, this point seems to me to be the most important. Sometimes we are afraid to ask because we think

---

16 Conf. Bajpai, G. S. / Kapoor, Neha, *Innovative Teaching Pedagogies in Law: A Critical Analysis of Methods and Tools* (March 31st, 2018) in: Contemporary Law Review, Vol. 2, 2018 (seen at https://ssrn.com/abstract=3172741 [01.06.2020]).
17 Conf. ibid.
18 Ibid.
19 Ibid.

that maybe the teacher will think, how is possible that they don't know such an easy thing. The fear of asking questions leads us to not get the answer and that leaves our knowledge incomplete. If there are gaps in the information provided, people will make assumptions about who should fill that gap, based on their prior knowledge. New information is more easily retained if one person has prior knowledge on which to add others. The more questions we ask the more knowledge we gain and so our memory will be filled with even more information.

## D. Teaching and learning techniques of law

One of the oldest teaching principles is that students have to learn on their own. Therefore, the job of the teacher is not so much in providing knowledge as in helping and guiding students. Teachers should help their students discover the very ideas and concepts behind the pages they read. Foreign students have more difficulties than locals to understand the lessons especially law vocabulary. Individuals are more likely to remember information if it is provided in a language that they understand and that it is easy to make a connection.

So if there is a complex issue to discuss, we students will understand better when we link it to something that happens in everyday life. Students remember better either with funny or interesting examples. People retrieve information using different senses such as watching for example or listening. If both of these senses are used, remembering information will be longer. When you hear some information and also look them written in a particular way or color, that information will be longer remembered.

Students should become familiar with the standards of legal thinking as soon and as efficiently as possible. I believe that innovative methods can be perfect tools for it. In legal education it often happens that students are not able to follow the material, since we as students are required to study a lot and we are struggling with the knowledge level of thinking. Therefore, the proper motivating, even encouraging students with the help of these methods are capable of promoting interest towards any given subject, as well as to try to find tasks that seem to be meaningful after the exams.[20]

---

20 Conf. Grosu, Manuela Renáta, *The Role of Innovative Teaching and Learning Methods in Legal Education*, https://conference.pixel-online.net/conferences/edu_future/common/download/Paper_pdf/ITL34-Grosu.pdf [01.06.2020]), p. 2.

Solving a problem smoothly and logically, step-by-step through the plain knowledge which has been delivered by the teacher seems exactly what legal education is about.[21] As Grosu would remark, "in this scenario the role of the student is to become a real problem solver who masters legal knowledge through more or less bounded problem solving"[22]. Furthermore though, a teacher's main task is to guide the student safely to knowledge and practically relevant case solutions.[23] That is because students simply need every possible opportunity in order to learn and also to practice themselves in regard especially to the legal profession.[24] Innovative methods can provide law students significant experience with practice and opportunities to deal with issues of legal profession. It is necessary that law faculty implements learning techniques that allow the student to understand what is, for instance a courtroom network and how the different individuals involved (e.g. judges, prosecutors, defendants, victims) interact with each other.

Another important innovative teaching method seeks for an encouraged students' collaboration in projects.[25] Collaboration has by its own right advanced to be an essential career and life skill.[26] Teachers can foster it in the classroom by making students to work in groups.[27] Professors of law are able to stimulate student learning through the implementation of certain communities of practice.[28] Through inclusive forms of communities of practice in the classroom students are helped to learn the course materials more thoroughly, which also provides for a pedagogical tool for teaching other skills needed in order to practice law.[29]

---

21  Conf. ibid.

22  Ibid.

23  Conf. ibid.; also Savin Baden, Maggi / Howell Major, Claire, *Foundations of Problem-Based Learning*, Maidenhead, 2004, pp. 3–9.

24  Conf. Grosu (op.cit.), p. 2; conf. also Sullivan, William M.; Colby, Anne; Welch Wegner, Judith; Bond, Lloyd; Shulman, Lee S., *Educating Lawyers: Preparation for the Profession of Law*, San Francisco 2007, p. 6.

25  Conf. N.N., *Innovative Methods of Teaching Strategies: That Will Help Every Teacher In The Claasroom* (February 25th, 2019), https://fedena.com/blog/2019/02/innovative-methods-of-teaching-strategies-that-will-help-every-teacher-in-the-classroom.html [01.06.2020].

26  Conf. ibid.

27  Conf. ibid.

28  Conf. Lockwood, Cristina D., *Improving learning in the law school classroom by encouraging students from communities of practice*, 20 Clinical Law Review (2013), pp. 95–135 (95).

29  Conf. ibid., p. 98.

Teachers need to get us to see right through possible problems and hypotheticals how a fact change can produce an outcome change.[30] Also to teaching us the analysis of cases by dissecting them, at the same time breaking them down into its various relevant components (among others facts, precedent, and application) in order to clarify what a court and its judges are actually doing.[31] Furthermore, they need to improve constantly our ability to understand the difference between crucial case facts and irrelevant ones.[32] The most important is to give us practical advise with regard to real world litigation.[33]

### Conclusion

Innovation is important to the advancement of society. It is important in any context. The efficiency you will gain through innovation is not something you can afford to overlook. The overall goal is to create knowledge and enhance learning in a positive classroom environment. Innovative methods can provide law students significant experience with practice and opportunities to deal with issues of legal profession. With the aid of innovative methods the deadlocks will break down and impasses that might occur during our learning process can be avoided. Innovation in education means finding any way a teacher can to reach all of their students. This means being willing and flexible to adjust what you as a teacher teach and how you teach. It is the quality of teachers approach inside any space that will make the biggest difference to their learners. As Alexandra K. Trenfor remarked, "The best teachers are those who show us where to look, but don't tell us what to see".[34] In conclusion, we as student want teacher's advices on the activities that we will develop. We want also that teachers accept the students' feedback on the method to be developed. Together we can do it.

---

30 Conf. Katz, Howard E. / O'Neill, Kevin Francis, *Strategies and Techniques of Law School Teaching. A Primer for New (and Not So New) Professors*, Austin/Boston/Chicago/New York/The Netherlands 2009, p. 3.
31 Conf. ibid.
32 Conf. ibid.
33 Conf. ibid.
34 See Dye, Allison, *Alexandra K. Trenfor Reminded Me of These Two Things* (June 28th, 2018, https://churchm.ag/alexandra-k-trenfor/ [01.06.2020].

# 'Jigsaw Classroom' and Law Teaching – Theoretical and Practical Implications from Modeled Lecture with 'Jigsaw Classroom'

*Kire Jovanov*[*]

The implementation of innovative teaching methods in legal education poses a quite interesting question regarding the sustainability of legal education itself. From student's perspective, the notion whether legal education accommodates their academic needs, highlights a discrepancy between the lecturer objectives and the student's needs. Since the lecturer's aspiration is to facilitate the group and to transmit the subject matter in a most suitable way, this interaction sometimes might come in odds with the very nature of legal education. This relationship perceived both from side of a lecturer and student, unfolds a broader perspective on the current state of mind in legal education, the need for change, and the theoretical and practical implications on the introduction/execution of 'Jigsaw Classroom' in the law classroom.

## A. Introduction

The special connection between the lecturers' aspiration of presenting the subject matter in a most pragmatic way and the students' need to comprehend the well-established principles of a legal system, collides sometimes with the interests of both the lecturer and the knowledge-starving student. Occasionally it might become difficult for a lecturer to adjust to the needs of the students, especially in present times, when students' expectations are at high level. Not only this difficulty exists from point of view of the lecturer but is consistently present also from the side of the student, since students expect a well-balanced approach of teaching and presenting the legal material by the lecturer in a way that would satisfy their academic needs.

---

[*] Kire Jovanov, LL.M. (Joint Degree Hanover / Lisbon / Rouen), Doctoral Candidate at the Faculty of Law, Gottfried Wilhelm Leibniz University Hanover.

Striking balance in this field is quite challenging for both the lecturer and the students. In order to elevate success in the law classroom, lecturers might make use of innovative methods of law teaching. Simultaneously, the students need to commit and interact within the introduced method so they can achieve the most out of it.

Following this argumentation, the 'Jigsaw Classroom' teaching method highlights the dependence of both the lecturer and the student in a way that in order the lecturer to achieve the pursued goal – presenting the complex legal material in a pragmatic way – it should strive to intensify teamwork between the members of the groups (in the law classroom)[1]. This interdependence, *inter alia*, is part of the research in the following work. The work itself follows an interdisciplinary research pattern, by intertwining educational theory and psychology with legal education. It is however my personal opinion, before enabling the academia to question and perceive the strengths/weaknesses of the introduction of such innovative teaching method into law teaching, it is important to address the question on the contemporariness of law teaching (Section B). Section C deals with the theoretical aspects of 'Jigsaw Classroom', whereas Section D illustrates the practicability of the introduction of this innovative teaching method in the framework of the lecture 'Introduction in Legal Writing'. The Outcomes (Section E) and the Conclusions (F) represent an integral part of this research paper.

I would like to express my sincere gratitude to Mr Jan Grosshennig (High School Teacher in Physics and Biology at Obeschule Westercelle – Celle/Germany) for his inspirational remarks in the period of constructing the lecture with 'Jigsaw Classroom' in August 2019 and for taking valuable time to provide me with educational theory and psychology literature.

## B. How Contemporary is Law Teaching?

Legal norms and legal methods form the entirety of law, but their vivid application into relations between social human beings brings a slightly more different approach regarding their essence. What can be understood under the term 'law'? Is it a technical system of understanding paragraphs

---

1 See more on the role of law teachers in the law classroom in: Heath, Mary / Galloway, Kate / Skead, Natalie / Steel, Alex / Israel, Mark, *Learning to Feel Like a Lawyer: Law Teachers, Sessional Teaching and Emotional Labour in Legal Education*, Griffith Law Review, 2018, p. 430–457 (433).

or is it an element in a set of tools helping to find legal solutions? *White* describes law as not being *"a set of rules at all, but a form of life"*[2], an understanding that intentionally brings the need for a more balanced approach in the process of transmitting legal material.

From a comparative perspective it is important to be noticed, especially in regard to the developments within law teaching in the United States ('US'), that US universities in the 19th century introduced a shift from *"passive transmission of static knowledge"* towards a *"much more active engagement with ideas"* , as *Coper* points out, particularly through the contributions of Harvard professor Langdell and his introduction of the *"casebook"* and the *"Socratic method"*.[3]

From European perspective, it is to be observed that the European legal education (with changes taking place following the signing of the Bologna Declaration[4] in 1999 and the incorporation of extra-curricular Moot Court competitions) has been locked in its rigid form and has showed less openness towards a more innovative approach[5] in regard to the process of law teaching. *Holgado Sáez / Ríos Corbacho* argue that the very important process behind the establishment of the European Higher Education Area itself, brought however changes to the university law classroom, hence embracing a slightly shift from the proactive role of the professor towards a proactive role of the student.[6] In this context it is quite challenging and to be critically questioned whether legal education has the needed ability to adjust to the societal transformations especially at university level.

From a slightly different angle, *Grosu* addresses the lack of an *"innovative approach"* as a consequence behind the main idea of legal education being a *"step-by-step logical problem-solving through knowledge"*[7] principle in order to establish well-educated law professionals that will become a *"problem solver[s]"*[8]. Rather than this, the argumentation should follow the line

---

2  White, James Boyd, *An Old-Fashioned View of the Nature of Law*, Theoretical Inquiries in Law 12 (1), 2011, p. 381–402 (382).

3  Coper, Michael, *Educating Lawyers for What? Reshaping the Idea of Law School*, Penn State International Law Review, 2010, p. 25–37 (29).

4  Joint Declaration of the European Ministers of Education (Bologna Declaration of 19 June 1999); See more in: Holgado Sáez, Christina / Ríos Corbacho, José Manuel, *El Espacio Europeo De Educación Superior: Técnicas Y Herramientas Colaborativas En El Derecho*, Dereito, 2009, p. 325–341 (326).

5  Grosu, Manuela Renáta, *The Role of Innovative Teaching and Learning Methods in Legal Education*, 2011, International Conference – Future of Education, Budapest.

6  Holgado Sáez / Ríos Corbacho (op.cit.), p. 327.

7  Grosu (op.cit.).

8  Ibid.

of the very essence behind the human's nature itself and its role in a given society, namely the knowledge of the society-based principles that should be transmitted in an academic environment[9] – at university level – in order to strengthen the students personal skills.[10] *Coper* argues that it is from pivotal importance that legal education transmits tools in order to equip and prepare the students *"for a life of service to the community in the best"*[11], rather than *"merely for a life of material personal success"*[12]. Therefore the already started shift within the legal education from one with a *"rigidly doctrinal focus"* towards one with a focus on the *"acquisition of skills, including the interpersonal and communication skills that students will require as graduates"*[13] should be intensified.

According to the abovesaid, a logical continuation of the argumentation brings a quite difficult question to the surface: *Shall the main essence of legal education be cored in the creation of a problem solver that is well-equipped with all methodological tools to pursue the best knowledge-based interpretation of legal norms or the focus shall be put also on the transmission of knowledge regarding the society-based principles connected to the interpretation of legal norms?* This challenging question goes beyond our need and desiderata to change (or adapt) our way of law teaching. Setting priorities in this sense would lead to a tectonic shift of paradigms, a process that at some point might favor a more sustainable option for the upcoming decades – *"advocate for rule of law"*[14].

## C. 'Jigsaw Classroom'

'Jigsaw Classroom' was developed in 1971 by the professor of psychology Elliot Aronson at the University of Texas in order to combat *"hostility among group of students [whites, African-Americans and Hispanics] who found themselves in the same classroom for the first time"*.[15] This teaching method

---

9 It is more than obvious that such principles are to be transmitted since the youngest of ages, however the transmission of such principles at university level by lecturers gives a totally different understanding behind these principles.
10 See more for a quite simmilar approach in: Coper (op.cit.), p. 30.
11 Ibid.
12 Ibid.
13 Heath / Galloway / Skead / Steel / Israel (op.cit.), p. 431.
14 Coper (op.cit.), p. 33.
15 Reese, Susan, *The Jigsaw Classroom*, Techniques, 2009, p. 8–9 (8); Holgado Sáez / Ríos Corbacho (op.cit.), p. 330.

enables an intensive engagement between students stimulating a change of perception towards other students, not only as competitors, but also as connecting links[16] who can help to achieve the learning goal.[17] In heterogeneous groups, taking into account the high level of differences in opinions, perspectives and value systems, research studies already shown that students benefit from the understanding of other students.[18] It is also important to be noticed, that not only combating impatience between different ethnic groups may be the only positive outcome of the application of the method, but rather as *Kirk* concludes in her research, that positive outcome is also evident in the subject-specific learning assignments of the students.[19] Relevant is also the argumentation of *Reese* stating that the smooth transition from competitiveness towards cooperation needs to take place in the classroom in order the general hostility between students to be diminished.[20] Some empirical researches show that students being part of a minority groups would have felt less intimidated within the 'Jigsaw Classroom' rather than in a traditional classroom environment.[21] Therefore cooperation as one of the most important outcomes of 'Jigsaw Classroom' elevates the need of the student to shift positions, namely from one of a passive listener, to an active thinker, hence becoming aware of different arguments and being intertwined with the group members.[22]

### D. Bringing 'Jigsaw Classroom' into the Law Classroom – Modeled Lecture (Introduction to Legal Writing)

In the framework of the lecture 'Introduction to Legal Writing' in the Summer Semester 2019, I decided to practically introduce and implement 'Jigsaw Classroom'. Firstly, my motivation to introduce this method to the law classroom was embodied through my experience gained as a PhD can-

---

16  Ibid; See more for: *"fuende de aprendizaje"* (learning sources).
17  Ibid.
18  Thyfault, Roberta K. / Fehrman, Kathryn, *Interactive Group Learning in the Legal Writing Classroom: An International Primer on Student Collaboration and Cooperation in Large Classrooms*, John Marshall Law Journal, 2009, p. 136–164 (144).
19  Kirk, Sabine, *48. Partner- und Gruppenarbeit*, in: Karl-Heinz Arnold / Uwe Sandfuchs / Jürgen Wiechmann (Ed.), Handbuch Unterricht, 2nd ed. Bad Heilbrunn 2009, p. 228, MN. 3.5; See more for a more methodological and practical implication in: Thyfault / Fehrman (op.cit.), p. 161.
20  Reese (op.cit.), p. 8.
21  Thyfault / Fehrman (op.cit.), p. 147.
22  Thyfault / Fehrman (op.cit.), p. 142.

didate, lecturer, and research student in a local law firm, which is why I was able to contribute on optimisation opportunities. Secondly, since the group of students that I was working with, were students having multi-cultural background and were coming from different legal orders, it become important to address not only the essence behind the writing process of legal scientific work in accordance with the writing requirements in Germany, but also to enhance empathy and teamwork between them. During my previous lectures it become evident for me that in the classroom a slightly academic rivalry was present[23], for which reason it become important for me to build an environment for all students to achieve the best possible outcome.

The lecture with the adoption of 'Jigsaw Classroom' was structured in the following way:

## I Phase: Brainstorming and Introduction

The first phase is divided in two sub-phases: the first sub-phase being brainstorming and the second sub-phase being introduction to the subject-matter in a form of giving oral input to the students.

Before commencing with the actual teaching method, I introduced brainstorming to address the main topics for the relevance of the lecture. From my perspective as lecturer, it was important to stimulate the students to actively participate in this phase, by finding initial keywords that will enable a more easier writing process of legal scientific works. From the student's perspective, it was more than relevant that the students possess enough material to prepare their work independently, so contribution could be made in the following discussions in the 'expert groups' and during the joint discussion.

I addressed the question regarding the most important elements of a scientific work to the plenum, so the students could start naming keywords relating to the main question. In this phase no prior input was given by myself, since I was expecting from the students to recall the material that we already completed in the previous weeks.

---

23  In this sense I would like to state, that I do not perceive academic rivalry among students as negative circumstance, rather than that it was my personal goal to enhance teamwork between students with a final outcome that every student works together in the groups so they can canalise their strengths for the purpose of the group.

Following the first sub-phase, my role changed from a 'moderator', to a lecturer that gives input. It was my personal intention to commence again facilitating the main understanding behind the findings in the first sub-phase. The second sub-phase aims at giving the lecturer once more the main role in the lecture taking into account that the main idea behind this sub-phase is giving input on the subject matter.[24] For the purpose of my lecture more precisely, input in a sense that the students will get enough material and background information on the subject matter so they can start to connect the findings from the first sub-phase with the input given by myself in the second sub-phase and continue to work together in groups in the following phases.

## II Phase: Expert Groups

After the conclusion of the first phase, I divided the students into three groups (the groups correspond to the main subjects of the topic that is to be discussed). According to the literature, these groups are called expert groups.[25] The division in this lecture followed the line of division of the main parts of a legal scientific work, namely <u>introduction</u>, <u>main part</u>, and <u>conclusions</u>. The first expert group was assigned with the introduction, the second with the main part and the third with the conclusions. Additionally, to this division, an assignment was given to the expert groups. The assignment was all about enhancing communication within the group, in order to establish a common ground for exchange of arguments in order as experts to find suitable keywords that will reflect the assigned part of one scientific work. Precisely this means that the students were given enough amount of time to explore the subject matter, to connect the initial keywords from the brainstorming to the acquired knowledge during my introduction and to commence working within the assigned expert group.

---

24  In this sense Holgado Sáez / Ríos Corbacho identify five main tasks that the lecturer should do within the "Jigsaw Classroom": 1) *selection of members of the Expert Groups*, 2) *choosing a subject matter*, 3) *giving input*, 4) *giving advice in correlation to the subject matter/assignment* and 5) *evaluation of the work of the puzzle*; see more in: Holgado Sáez / Ríos Corbacho (op.cit.), p. 331.
25  Ibid, p. 333; *"temporary expert groups"* in: Reese (op.cit.), p. 9.

## III Phase: Mixed Groups

Following the conclusion of this assignment, the members of the expert groups needed to change places and become part of different expert groups. These allows the students in their role as experts in their field to exchange their views on a certain topic and to learn from other experts about the topics that are not being discussed by themselves. Therefore, during the second and third phase it is expected from the students to actively engage in the work of the group, since otherwise they would not have any material to address in the other group.

## IV Phase: Joint Discussion

In the last phase of 'Jigsaw Classroom' all groups are being dissolved and the lecture continued as a joint discussion between all students and myself. In this phase, I resumed my role of moderator, and together with the students highlighted the main outcomes of the lecture.

The illustration of 'Jigsaw Classroom' has the following pattern:

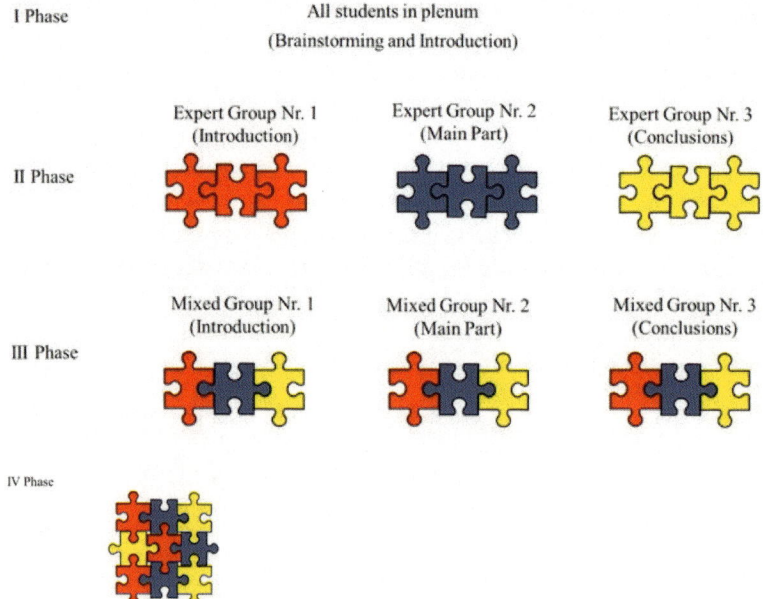

Own illustration based on *Langfeldt*, Psychologie für die Schule, 2006, p. 153.

## C. Outcomes

The process of conceptualisation of a lecture with 'Jigsaw Classroom' according to my personal experience do not create many challenges, rather than that it is quite easy in the preparation and the execution. The flexibility of the method comes with the allocation of as many as needed subject matters and groups, that according to the lecturer's needs can be adjusted. In this sense, the lecturer can decide in how many groups the plenum will be divided and which subject matters each of the expert groups will deal with. Important remark is however the process of changing the composition of the expert groups towards the mixed groups according to the above illustration, since otherwise there would be no incentive left to the student to participate in the work of the expert groups. Following the argumentation by *Holgado Sáez / Ríos Corbacho*, I also argue that at the beginning there is a certain amount of difficulty when the method is introduced, since the students are sceptical (or even not interested) to participate in the team.[26] To what extent this notion might be corelating to the very specific nature of legal education is unfortunately not clearly answered in the literature. Such examination would bring further empirical research on the matter, especially by incorporating the method in different law disciplines i.e. civil, penal, and public law. My personal observation shows that there is a fragmented understanding about cooperation in the law classroom. It is therefore the task of the lecturer to stimulate cooperation, by introducing additional assignments that focus on enhancing cooperation. Some studies also show that through the process of learning by doing students learn the most, since they are practically exposed to the specific material.[27]

## D. Conclusions

Legal education follows a quite rigid form of transmitting law in the University law classroom, although (as the content of this research work unfolded) it can be perceived that there are straightforward actions and changes that are taking place, particularly in Europe. In present times, marked by social transformation, especially regarding digitalisation, students might tend to scrutinize "old-fashioned" way of transmitting law. The question that must be answered at this point, is whether law teaching

---

26  Holgado Sáez / Ríos Corbacho (op.cit.), p. 330.
27  Thyfault / Fehrman (op.cit.), p. 136.

is "old-fashioned" or not? Following the argumentation in this research work, it can be concluded that law teaching at some point it might be characterised as "old-fashioned", yet it is also important to be noticed that the difficulty behind transmitting the legal material poses challenges and risks when applying different innovative teaching methods. However, this does not pose an obstacle for new innovative methods of teaching to be introduced in the law classroom.

This research work outlined several contemporary literature observations and concluded that law in a matter of fact should be perceived as a form of life and therefore treated in that manner. This means that the process of transmitting law should also follow a pattern that changes simultaneously with the changes taking place in each society. Therefore, social elements such as inclusion, cooperation, multi-culturalism etc. should be emphasised at every stage of the legal education.

In this sense the introduction of 'Jigsaw Classroom' into 'Introduction to Legal Writing' contributed to strengthen empathy and teamwork between students, through a process of learning by doing. Moreover, the research work showed through its practical element that the introduction and execution of the said method are characterised with less complexity, hence displaying high flexibility and adjustment of the method to the needs of the lecturer and students.

# The Flipped Classroom Approach in Legal Education

*Arndt Künnecke*[*]

When I already had been working at some private university in Istanbul for almost seven years, I received an offer to join the Law faculty of a brand-newly founded university in Istanbul called MEF. In my first meeting with the Dean of the Law faculty I was told that this newly founded university was not just another university on the big market of private universities in Turkey, but that it had a unique feature: the *Flipped Classroom*. I never heard about a "flipped classroom" before, so I thought it might be some special feature concerning the architectural design of the classroom. But then I was told that *Flipped Classroom* was a teaching approach being developed in the USA some years ago. And this new university planned to practise this *Flipped Classroom* approach comprehensively in all faculties, courses and lessons. Sounded interesting to me, however, what was this *Flipped Classroom* model the university wanted to fully implement as the first university worldwide?[1]

## A. *What is the* Flipped Classroom?

To start with, there is no universal definition of the term *"Flipped Classroom"*. Reading some descriptions and articles about the *Flipped Classroom* it turns out that it generally provides a pre-recorded introductory lecture (video and/or audio) which is followed by some in-class activities. The students watch and/or listen to this pre-class lecture somewhere outside the classroom and in time before the class starts. When they come to class, they are already equipped with some basic knowledge about the topic of the class so that the freed in-class time can be used for interactive tasks,

---

[*] Prof. Dr. Dr. Arndt Künnecke, Federal University of Applied Sciences for Public Administration Brühl / Germany.
1 Şahin, Muhammed / Fell Kurban, Caroline, *The New University Model*, Houston 2019, p. 52.

such as exercises, discussions, Q&A sessions or other learning activities.[2] Flipping the classroom in this sense means changing the process of traditional teaching: Instead of introducing the students the topic physically in class and giving them follow-up tasks for home, the teacher already gives them a pre-class introduction and builds on that basic knowledge to guide the students through learning activities in class which helps them getting a deeper understanding of the topic. A cohort of more than 100 flipped learning instructors from nearly 50 countries came together in 2018 and created an updated definition of *Flipped Classroom*. According to their definition, "*the flipped approach inverts the traditional classroom model by introducing course concepts before class, allowing educators to use time to guide each student through active, practical, innovative applications of the course principles*"[3]. In short, taking into account the technical means being used for its realisation, *Flipped Classroom* can be defined as "*any teaching model which replaces in-class lecture modules with video or audio lectures with the goal to use the freed in-class time for interactivity*"[4].

---

2  Compare Centre for Academic Development and Quality, Nottingham Trent University, *CADQ Guide – The Flipped Classroom* (June 2013), retrieved from www.ntu.ac.uk/adq [15.04.2020]; Davis, Laurel E. / Neary, Mary Ann / Vaughn, Susan E., *Teaching Advanced Legal Research in a Flipped Classroom*, in: 22 Perspectives: Teaching Legal Research and Writing (2013), p. 13; Educause Learning Initiative, *7 Things you should know about Flipped Classrooms*, retrieved from http://net. educause.edu/ir/library/pdf/eli7081.pdf [15.04.2020]; Lihosit, Judith / Larrington, Jane, *Flipping the Legal Research Classroom*, in: 22 Perspectives Teaching Legal Research and Writing (2013), p. 1; Slomanson, William R., *Blended Classroom: A Flipped Classroom Experiment at the Lectern*, in: Journal of Legal Education 64 (2014–15), p. 95; Upchurch, Angela, *Optimizing the Law School Classroom through the 'Flipped' Classroom Model*, in: The Law Teacher (Fall 2013), p. 1.

3  The Flipped Learning Global Initiative (n. d.), retrieved from http://www.flglobal. org [15.04.2020].

4  Wolff, Lutz-Christian / Chan, Jenny, *Flipped Classrooms for Legal Education*, Singapore 2016, p. 13.

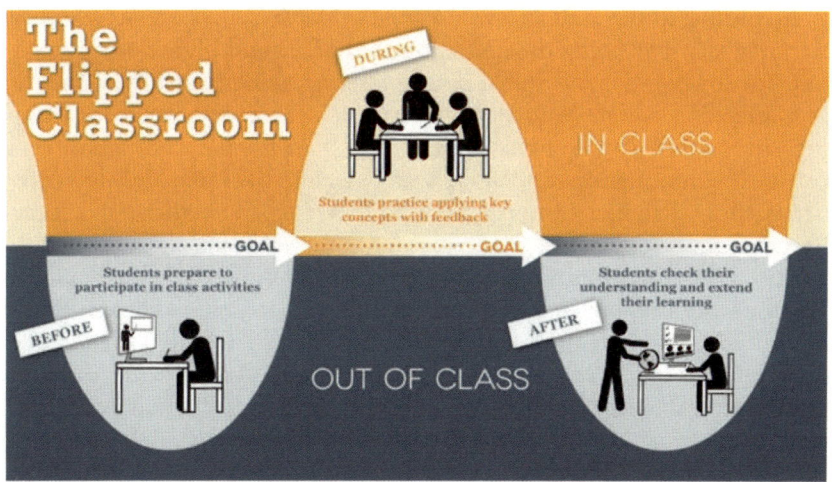

Source: https://facultyinnovate.utexas.edu/sites/default/files/flippedgraphic(web960px).png

The origins of the *Flipped Classroom* teaching approach go back to the year 2007 when two high school teachers in the US, Jonathan Bergmann and Aaron Sams, were concerned about more and more of their students missing classes for several reasons. To give them a chance to catch up, both began to record lectures and presentations which they made available for their students on YouTube.[5] In 2012 they published a book *Flip Your Classroom: Reach Every Student in Every Class Every Day*, in which they introduced their approach of providing the students pre-class videos.[6] One year later, in 2013, research was published comparing flipped and traditional courses. They found out that flipped courses had higher student satisfaction and success rate than the traditional ones.[7]

---

5 Hamdan, Noora / McKnight, Patrick et al., *The Flipped Learning Model: A White Paper based on the Literature Review titled a review of Flipped Learning* (2013), p.3, retrieved from https://flippedlearning.org/wp-content/uploads/2016/07/WhitePaper_FlippedLearning.pdf, pp. 9 [15.04.2020].

6 Bergmann, Jonathan / Sams, Aaron, *Flip Your Classroom: Reach Every Student in Every Class Every Day*, Washington D. C. 2012.

7 Davies, Randy S. / Dean, Douglas L. / Ball, Nick, *Flipping the Classroom and Instructional Technology Integration in a College-Level Information Systems Spreadsheet Course*, in: Educational Technology Research and Development 61 (4) 2013, pp. 578.

According to the well-known *Bloom's Taxonomy*, there are six levels of learning activities being divided into lower-order and higher-order activities. The lower-order activities are remembering, understanding and applying, whereas the higher-order activities are analysing, evaluating and creating.[8] In traditional classrooms, where teachers merely have enough time to convey the information needed for understanding the topic, only lower-order learning activities can be conducted.[9] Among the higher-order learning activities would be the preparation of homework, writing legal memoranda or case solutions, or doing assigned research work. In a traditional classroom setting, not many students would get engaged in these high-order learning activities and consequently, the overall learning output would remain rather low.[10] In contrast to that, in *Flipped Classrooms* the lower-order learning activities, such as remembering, understanding and applying, take place before and outside the classroom, when the students listen to the audio introduction or watch the pre-class introductory video.[11] Therefore, the teacher can make use of the freed-up classroom time for getting the students engaged in higher-order learning activities, such as analysing, evaluating and creating the content which was already delivered before meeting face-to-face in the classroom. Fostering these activities is of special importance for Law classes, as they enable the students to develop and practise critical thinking and to use the skills they acquired by listening to the audio or by watching the video introduction to the lesson.[12]

---

8 See in detail: Krathwohl, David R., *A Revision of Bloom's Taxonomy: An Overview*, in: THEORY INTO PRACTICE, Volume 41, Number 4, Autumn 2002, pp. 212–218.
9 Lihosit / Larrington, *Flipping the Legal Research Classroom*, p. 3.
10 Lihosit / Larrington, *Flipping the Legal Research Classroom*, p. 3.
11 Lihosit / Larrington, *Flipping the Legal Research Classroom*, p. 4.
12 Lihosit / Larrington, *Flipping the Legal Research Classroom*, p. 4.

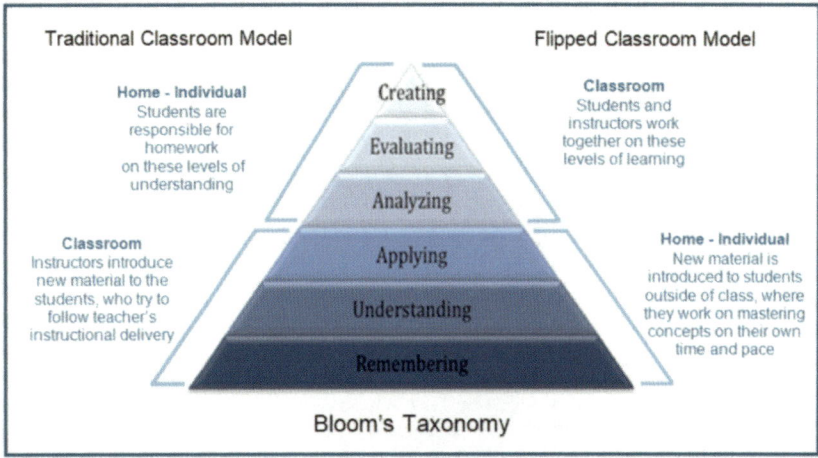

Source: https://www.researchgate.net/figure/Connection-between-Traditional-and-Flipped-Classroom-to-Blooms-Taxonomy_fig2_323900654

This is the theory. But how does *Flipped Classroom* teaching work in practice? And why it is considered being more effective than traditional teaching? This is something I would like to examine and explain from my own experience, having practised this teaching method from fall term 2014 on in my Law classes at MEF University in Istanbul.

Link to my explanatory video about *Flipped Classroom* at MEF University

## B. *How does the* Flipped Classroom *work in practice?*

In the traditional way, lectures and seminars are held as follows: The lecturer stands in front of the class and explains the topic, the students listen passively. The *Flipped Classroom* approach flips the classroom and turns the traditional classroom setting upside down. Now the students become the active part of the lessons, not the teacher. But before the students can become active, the teacher has to do his or her homework. He or she has to develop and implement a concept to prepare the students for the lesson. How that works can be explained in 7 steps:

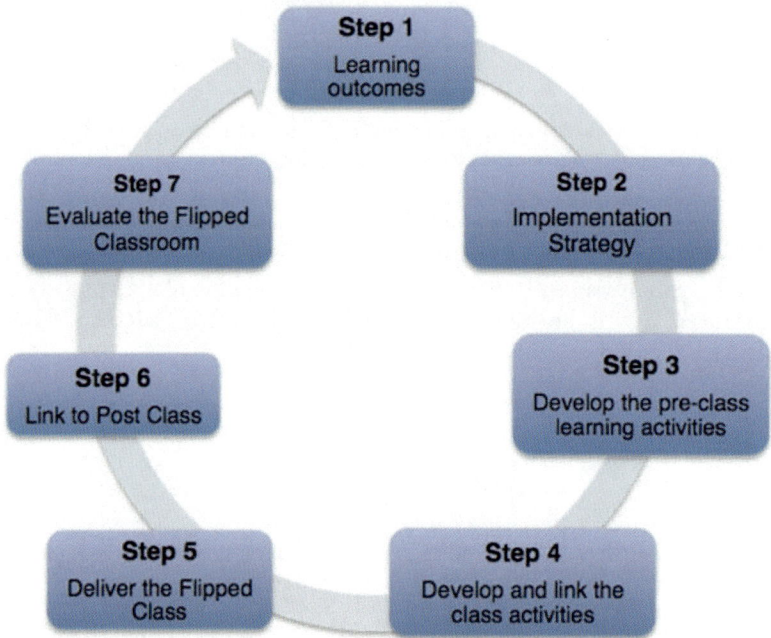

**Step 1:** First of all, the teacher has to define the learning outcomes of the lesson. This is done by clearly stating what the students are expected to be able to do and know about the topic at the completion of the lesson. The set learning outcomes not only serve the purpose of directing the content and design of the flipped lesson, they form the basis of the later evaluation of the *Flipped Classroom* lesson.

 **Step 2:** After having set the learning outcomes for the lesson, the teacher has to develop a strategy for implementing these set learning outcomes.

The most difficult task here is to decide which input should be given before, during and after meeting the students in the classroom. In other words, the teacher must didactically divide the topics to be taught into three parts: pre-class learning activities, in-class activities and post-class reinforcing activities.

**Step 3:** The core feature of the pre-class activities of the *Flipped Classroom* teaching approach are the introductory videos/audios. Therefore, as the next step, a concept has to be developed that defines which part of the topic is suitable to be explained in a pre-class video or audio. As the basis for the in-class activities has to be established in advance, the introductory video or audio needs to understandably introduce a legal term, concept, problem or case in short. Ideally, the big idea of the lesson should be included in the video/audio, easy to understand and to remember for each student. The way we did that at MEF University was mainly by producing introductory videos of 5–15 min length for each lesson. Here it is important to mention, that no matter if you opt for audio or video, the recordings should not be too long and they should not try to replace the whole lecture. This material is only the introductory part of the *Flipped Classroom* lesson. Evaluations, not only at MEF University, showed that the attention span of the students watching and/or listening to content delivered online is restricted to maximum 15–20 min.[13] Keeping the video or audio short and to the point – that is the key to keep the student's attention.

For making a decision between recording a video or only an audio introduction, one needs to take into account not only the available technical equipment but also the effectiveness of both options. From the pedagogical point of view, there is no clear answer whether audio or video is the better means for delivering a pre-class introduction. It all depends on the different learning styles of the students.[14] However, in comparison to audios, videos have the big advantage that they appeal to more senses than just audio. As some students prefer reading, some listening and some others watching, videos include all three of these learning preferences: They

---

13　Davis / Neary / Vaughn, *Teaching Advanced Legal Research in a Flipped Classroom*, p. 14; Ireland, Jennifer, *Blended Learning in Intellectual Property: The Best of Both Worlds*, in: Legal Education Review 18 (2008), p. 150; Le Brun, Marlene / Johnstone, Richard, *The Quiet Revolution: Improving Student Learning in Law*, Sydney 1994, p. 260; McKellar, Patricia / Maharg, Paul, *Virtual learning environments: The alternative to the box under the bed*, in: The Law Teacher 39 (2005), p. 48; Şahin / Fell Kurban, *The New University Model*, p.157; Upchurch, *Optimizing the Law School Classroom through the 'Flipped' Classroom Model*, p. 5.

14　Wolff / Chan, *Flipped Classrooms for Legal Education*, p. 52.

offer text and pictures for the visual needs and sound and speech for the audio needs. So, the audio-visual content of videos serves the different needs of students more comprehensively than only audio or visual content. And it gives the teacher many more means to deliver his/her content.

However, before coming to my own experiences with pre-class videos, let me present you some general considerations concerning the audio and the video approach: Audios are definitely easier to produce and need less equipment and technology than videos.[15] They also allow the students to multitask, by giving them the chance to read additional topic-related material while listening to the audio recording.[16] But pre-class introductions only based on audio lack in developing any bonding with the teacher prior to the face-to-face sessions in class.

For producing pre-class videos, there are three main ways: the 'screen capture approach', the 'white board approach' and the 'green screen approach'. In the screen capture approach, the teacher creates a visual presentation, such as PowerPoint, Pdf or a Word document, and records his or her voice while showing and running the presentation or document on the computer. The video then shows the movement of the presentation or document on the computer screen synced with the recorded audio of the teacher.[17] For this kind of recording, screen capture software such as *Camtasia* or *Snagit*, which are quite easy to handle, can be used. In contrast to that, in the white board approach, the teacher films him- or herself in front of a white board, flip chart or screen.[18] In the green screen approach, the teacher tapes him- or herself in front of a green screen. The advantage of the screen capture is that a PowerPoint slideshow and the audio recording can be played simultaneously on the students' device, serving both visual and auditory learning styles. In addition, it is relatively easy to update certain parts of the recording, just by changing some slides and re-recording the related audio part.[19] This is rather difficult in the white board and green screen approach. Even for updating a small part of the content, the entire video has to be re-recorded, unless the teacher could appear in front of the camera again in the exact same style and outfit as in the original

---

15 Compare Martin, Peter W., *Cornell's experience running online, inter-school Law courses – an FAQ*, in: The Law Teacher 39 (2005), p. 79.
16 Ireland, *Blended Learning in Intellectual Property: The Best of Both Worlds*, p. 149.
17 Upchurch, *Optimizing the Law School Classroom through the 'Flipped' Classroom Model*, p. 3.
18 Upchurch, *Optimizing the Law School Classroom through the 'Flipped' Classroom Model*, p. 3.
19 Wolff / Chan, *Flipped Classroom for Legal Education*, p. 50.

video. Inserting an update with a teacher looking different to the appearance in the original video would make the whole video look unprofessional and not convincing. Therefore, to avoid needless updates, it is strongly recommended to avoid any unnecessary update references, for example to the names of persons holding a specific office, as they can change, and in that case make the whole video look outdated. The advantage of the white board and green screen approaches is the personal touch which is created when the teacher appears on screen him- or herself and directly speaks to the students.[20] As with pre-class introductions only based on audio, the screen capture approach is lacking in developing this personal bonding with the teacher prior to the face-to-face sessions in class. However, it is very important for the teacher to feel comfortable with appearing in front of the camera and to stay authentic. I have seen many colleagues who do not feel comfortable in front of a camera speaking to invisible students. This is something you can see from the first moment on watching their videos that they feel uncomfortable and lose their way in front of the camera. In this case it is strongly advised to use the screen capture approach or to simply use audio only. It will suit the personality of the teacher much better. But this not only counts for the pre-class introductory options where the teacher is not visible. Also, when the teacher decides to appear in front of the camera, it is very important that he or she stays authentic. The students know their teachers and see them regularly in class. Therefore, they expect their teacher to be the same person in class and in front of the camera. If the teacher tries to be someone else in front of the camera it will irritate the students and diminish the credibility of the teacher's message on video, unless he or she plays a certain role for didactical reasons.

According to my own experience of more than three years teaching following the *Flipped Classroom* approach at MEF University, the most effective way to deliver pre-class content in the form of videos aiming at attracting the students and keeping their attention is the advanced green screen approach: Record yourself in front of a green screen, talk to your students while looking in the camera and addressing them directly. This puts the teacher in the centre of their attention and will make students feel as if the teacher is communicating the message only to them. Seeing the teacher in person on video also creates a familiar and comfortable classroom atmosphere for your students as they know you as their teacher and instructor of the course. Using a green screen as background of your video shooting also enables you to place yourself in the scene of the topic when you ex-

---

20  Wolff / Chan, *Flipped Classroom for Legal Education*, p. 50, fn. 382.

change the green background with a photo or picture. In other words: You can already visually connect yourself and your message with the topic you explain and thereby create a setting which you would not be able to create inside the classroom. For example, when you explain some procedural rules of court proceedings, place yourself in a courtroom, when you explain something about the composition or competences of the EU Commission, place yourself right in front of the Commission building in Brussels. Also make use of written text in your videos, for example by slides or pop-ups including some keywords or short headlines corresponding with the things you are explaining. That visually underlines the core content of your introduction and helps the students to keep these points in mind. And, if possible, also try to include some interactive elements in your video, for example by interspersing some questions inside the video or by using tools like *Zaption* or *EDpuzzle* for adding images, text, quiz questions and discussions to existing videos. These little technical effects will have a big impact on how effectively the students receive and keep in mind your explanations. In order to provide all teachers these opportunities of technical support for their videos, MEF University had its own little studio with camera, green screen and lighting. In this studio, every teacher could record his or her own videos for the lessons. These introductory videos, which prepare the students for their classes, must be made available for the students some days before the actual lesson in the classroom. The easiest way to distribute the material to the students is to upload the videos on the university's learning platform. As nearly all universities use online learning platforms now for enrolment of the students in each course and for providing them additional course material, it is the best place to store the pre-class videos in a folder on that university-run platform. For example, at MEF University, we used the *Blackboard* System. It is a learning platform, a kind of university intranet, in which teachers and students find all necessary information about their courses, including the syllabus, the course content, the dates of the lessons, announcements, assessments and all necessary material for their classes, including the introductory *Flipped Classroom* videos. From that moment on, when the introductory video is uploaded and made available for the students, the students become the active part. However, they still need the support of the teacher on that stage.

At the beginning of each course, the teacher needs to teach the students how to view the pre-class videos effectively. This has to be done right at the beginning of each course, otherwise the whole idea of effectively practising the *Flipped Classroom* will fail as most of the students do not have any experience with this approach.[21] Especially, the students need to become familiar with using the videos/audios as a learning tool. Therefore, they should experience how to grasp the main content of each video/audio by using pause, go back and replay (parts of) the video/audio, in order to make their notes. This should be demonstrated by the teacher in the first lesson of the course when all students meet in the classroom for the first time.

With the uploaded pre-class video or audio, plus some additional material, the students are equipped with the information they need to work on the forthcoming topics on their own in the so-called individual space. The uploaded materials provide them an introduction to the lesson, explain the main content and give them short assignments preparing them for and making them curious about the forthcoming face-to-face lesson in the classroom. In fact, this approach means more work for both parties, the students and the teachers. The students have to watch the videos before each lesson, make some notes and think about the topic. Beyond the more time-consuming preparation, the teachers also need to be available for the students before class, to help them and answer their questions concerning the pre-class videos, materials and assignments either via e-mail, group space on the university's learning platform, or during the office hours.[22] However, the teachers should always keep in mind not to overload the students with pre-class work. Watching an introductory video or listening to an audio before class, plus perhaps reading some additional material and doing some pre-class assignment is already lots of work for the students.[23] Therefore, the pre-class workload for the students should be kept short and simple, in order to motivate and not frustrate them.

If some additional materials and/or assignments are added to the introductory video, they need to be clearly and understandably connected with the video. This can easily be done by referring to these materials or by introducing an assignment already inside the video. Ideally, the legal term, concept, problem, or case being introduced in the pre-class video or audio should be reinforced in assigned links or reading. Questions should also be included in the individual space before class. This can be done on three stages: before the video, inside the video and after the video. The purpose of pre-video questions is to activate some background knowledge of the

---

21 Şahin / Fell Kurban, *The New University Model*, p. 158.
22 Şahin / Fell Kurban, *The New University Model*, p. 170.
23 Redmond, Paul / Roper, Christopher, *Legal Education and Training in Hong Kong Preliminary Review: Summary of Consultation Paper (2000)*, pp. 22, 25 & 35, retrieved from http://www.hkLawsoc.org.hk [17.04.2020]; Wolff / Chan, *Flipped Classroom for Legal Education*, p. 59.

students and activate their understanding of what will come. Questions inside the video are meant to support the retrieval process by checking the students' understanding and remembering. Questions after the video enable the students to already think about how to use the information being provided in the video for the in-class time, for the whole course and for their future legal practice.[24] The idea behind using questions of any of these types on the pre-class level is that the students will increase the transfer of the given information into their long-term memory by doing short retrievals during their learning process. This effect is scientifically proven by the learning strategy of retrieval practice.[25]

**Step 4:** The most important part of the *Flipped Classroom* still takes place inside the classroom when teacher and students meet face-to-face. Therefore, it is crucial for the teacher to carefully develop and link class activities with the pre-class part . As the pre-class work provided understanding and memory of the introduced topic it was only meant to prepare the students for the in-class time. This approach can be compared to training a football team: The training sessions and the warm-up before the match only serve to prepare the team for the match. The truth lies on the pitch. The same logic applies to the *Flipped Classroom*: The time in the classroom shows if the students have understood and internalised the topic and if they are able to apply, analyse and evaluate it for their studies. The *Flipped Classroom's* pitch is the classroom. This is the group space where common activity takes place that shows some result at the end. As in football, there are some general tactics which are commonly practised on the pitch, the same applies in the classroom. These should not be the same in every classroom as the topic as well as the group of students are always different. Just as a football manager has to prepare his or her team for a single match against a special opponent, the teacher has to prepare the special group of students for a specific topic of a single lesson. Therefore, the teacher has to make sure that the chosen pre-class materials and assignments fit with the learning activities in class. In other words: The chosen in-class activity tools must be built upon the pre-class preparation and be suitable for using the acquired knowledge for deepening the topic inside the classroom. In gen-

24  Compare Şahin / Fell Kurban, *The New University Model*, p. 160.
25  Agarwal, Pooja K. / Roediger, Henry L. III. / McDaniel, Mark A. / McDermott, Kathleen B., *How to Use Retrieval Practice to Improve Learning*, St. Louis 2013, p. 4, retrieved from https://firstliteracy.org/wp-content/uploads/2015/07/RetrievalPracti ceGuide-for-FL-Workshop-on-Brain-Based-ESOL-Instruction.pdf [17.04.2020].

eral, there are three categories of active learning which can be used inside the classroom: guided practice, peer tutoring and small group work.[26]

Before practising any specific activity from these categories, the teacher is strongly advised to start the lesson with a short review activity making sure that the students remember and understand the concepts being presented in the pre-class video or audio. This can be done by asking the students to quickly discuss the essence of the information that they acquired prior to class in small groups and then present them to the class. This makes them review the key discourse and concepts among themselves first before they are encouraged to show their findings to the teacher.[27] It also offers the teacher the opportunity to correct any misunderstandings of the topic before starting with the learning activities inside the classroom. Instead of starting-off with a short review unit, especially in Law classes, the teacher can also start the lesson with a topic-related problem issue based on a real-life example that has to be discussed by the students first in small groups and later on in the whole class. This approach also builds upon the knowledge acquired prior to class and immediately enforces the students to apply this knowledge in real-life scenarios.[28]

**Step 5:** After having successfully connected the pre-class preparation with the in-class topic by means of a start-of-unit, it is time for delivering the flipped class. As this face-to-face time with the group of students forms the core of active learning, this time should be effectively used. In order to enable the students to actively learn and not to listen passively, the teacher needs to be aware of his or her role inside the *Flipped Classroom*: The teacher's role shifts from transferring information by lecturing to providing the students with activities and exercises that help them to assimilate and apply what they have learned in the pre-class preparation. The teacher is still the expert in class, however, he or she is not supposed to present expert knowledge but to provide guided practice to the students, generate critical thinking and moderate activities and discussions.[29]

In Law classes, there are several active learning strategies that can be practised by each teacher inside the *Flipped Classroom*. Here I would only like to shortly introduce a few of them:

The *peer instruction* strategy is a strategy even suitable for larger groups. The teacher asks the students some questions based on the pre-class work.

---

26 Şahin / Fell Kurban, *The New University Model*, p. 221.
27 Şahin / Fell Kurban, *The New University Model*, pp. 213.
28 Şahin / Fell Kurban, The New University Model, p. 221.
29 Şahin / Fell Kurban, *The New University Model*, p. 212.

After giving them some time to think, the students' task is to debate their answers to the questions in small groups or altogether in class. The challenge for the students is to convince their peers with their arguments. For the teacher this offers the opportunity to understand more about the students' thinking process as they still develop their arguments and answers in the discussion.[30]

The *Socratic seminar* strategy is similar to this peer instruction strategy. According to this approach, the teacher leaves the students with an open-ended question based on the pre-class introduction to discuss in group(s). Here, the focus is not on debating different points of view but on understanding the legal term, concept or problem by discussing it in a lively rather than a controversial manner. The purpose is to get the students discussing an idea or issue more in depth and taking the responsibility for the setup of the discussion themselves. The teacher should only give the initial question and then stay outside the discussion. His or her role is the position of a spectator who gets a better idea about the students' speaking skills and comprehension of the topic just by observing the discussion and the students' contributions to it.[31]

*Case studies* are another active learning strategy suitable for Law classes. After the pre-class introduction of a specific legal term, concept or problem, the students are presented with a case and an open-ended question which they have to answer based on the case.[32] First, each student should try to find his or her own answer or hypothesis. Then, the students are divided into small groups in which they should discuss their findings. The task for each group is to find a consensus on the answer or hypothesis, that, as the next step, has to be presented in class for further discussion. These case studies combine problem-based and team-based learning. They hold each student accountable for the pre-work and encourage them to present and discuss their ideas in a small group. Same as in peer instruction, the teacher can walk around and listen to parts of each group discussion to have an idea about the students' thinking process and abilities to argue.

Another active learning strategy is the strategy of *inquiry*. This is especially useful for sharpening the students' minds for important judicial arguments or court decisions. To carry out an inquiry, the teacher gives the

---

30  See in detail: Mazur, Eric, *Peer Instruction: A User's Manual*, upper Saddle River 1997, pp. 9.
31  Şahin / Fell Kurban, *The New University Model*, pp. 236.
32  Vanderbilt University Center for Teaching, *Cases Studies*, retrieved from https://cft .vanderbilt.edu/guides-sub-pages/case-studies/ [18.04.2020].

students the task to do some research on a rather specific and complex topic by either using their smartphones and laptops inside the classroom or by using the university library during class time. During the time of the students' research, the teacher should walk around and monitor if the students are on the right path with their inquiry. At the end of the research, the students are asked to present their findings and explain their research method to the whole group followed by a discussion. This strategy is quite similar to some types of pre-class work, with the difference that it is taking place in the middle of the group space. It can be practised from time to time, as it triggers the students' curiosity and helps them gain experience how to carry out small research tasks successfully.[33]

A completely different strategy for active learning is the *role play* or *simulation* strategy. This strategy simulates a situation or setting of the real world and makes the students enter into a role and act as if they are someone else. It is a very effective strategy in Law classes focusing on procedural Law and the practical application of Law. The most popular role-playing simulation is the Moot Court.[34] Moot courts are academic simulations of appellate advocacy. Students, acting as Lawyers or judges, simulate a case before an appellate court. In addition to acting as Lawyers or judges, students can also be assigned to serve as other parties to the proceedings, as Law clerks or reporters.[35] This setting of a court simulation allows students not only to bring in their factual knowledge but also encourages them to identify themselves with their roles and the setting and to reveal other talents, including emotions. Beyond that, it gives the teacher the possibility to get the whole class involved, if it is by playing a role in the simulation or by watching it and giving feedback afterwards. Each student will benefit from judging the case from different perspectives. However, to make such a Moot Court simulation a success, it is very important to give the students clear instructions and sufficient background beforehand and to make sure that there is enough time after the simulation for peer feedback among the students as well as for specific expert feedback by the teacher.[36] If this can-

---

33  Şahin / Fell Kurban, *The New University Model*, pp. 232.
34  Deardorff, Michelle Donaldson / Aliotta, Jilda, *Playing justice: The role of simulation in teaching and assessing the teaching of public Law*, in: Annual Meeting of the American Political Science Association, Washington DC, 2000.
35  Knerr, Charles R. / Sommerman, Andrew B., *Bringing the court into the undergraduate classroom: Appellate simulation in American college*, in: Laws and Courts 11 (2001), p. 4.
36  Şahin / Fell Kurban, *The New University Model*, pp. 234.

not be provided then the whole simulation would not have any measurable learning effect on the students and it would be a waste of time.

Another very different active learning strategy is the strategy of *gamification*.[37] At first sight, gamification might sound inappropriate for Law classes. This is true if it comes to fill the whole in-class time with this strategy. However, gamification is an entertaining and effective strategy as class-opener or for the closure of the lesson. It can be used as a motivating and at the same time competitive instrument to check the students' understanding of the topic. As an opener, the teacher could start the lesson with a short quiz, asking the students some multiple-choice questions concerning the content of the pre-class work. This could be done by using one of the freely accessible game-based online learning platforms such as *Kahoot!*. The teacher only has to prepare some quiz Q&As there beforehand and then the students can enter the quiz on their smartphones, tablets or laptops with the provided link and password. When the teacher opens a question, the students have to click on the correct answer as quickly as possible. Results are shown on the teacher's device, which is ideally connected with a monitor or screen being visible in class so that everybody can see who clicked on the right answer the quickest and how many students chose the correct answer. This form of checking the remembering and understanding the information which had been provided prior to class is not only an entertaining way of self-monitoring for each student, including a fun-factor and some competitiveness, but it also offers the teacher the opportunity to monitor how well the students understood and remembered the introduced pre-class content. The same effect can be achieved by using this gamification strategy at the end of the in-class time to check if all students reached the learning objectives of the lesson.

If and how effectively a teacher can practise any of these active learning strategies not only depends on him or her but also on the architecture and the equipment of the *Flipped Classroom*. For practising the *Flipped Classroom* at MEF University, the university chose a classroom design which remarkably deviated from the design of a normal classroom. The podium was placed in the middle of the classroom and groups of tables for six persons each were situated around the podium, all equipped with electric sockets, WIFI and direct links to the smartboard. As the teacher was not supposed to give a lecture anymore, he or she did not stand in front of the class anymore. Being placed right in the middle of the room without any physical boundaries to the students, the teacher became part of the class

---

37  Şahin / Fell Kurban, *The New University Model*, pp. 238.

and the environment, which perfectly reflects the teacher's role in the *Flipped Classroom* setting. Right from the beginning of each lesson, the students were automatically placed around the tables in small groups. This setting was already pre-planned for the learning activities which were mainly conducted in small groups. Apart from the technical equipment, the students could also make use of the specially painted walls of the classroom, being covered with a paint that turned them into whiteboards. That enabled them to write down the results of their group work on the walls and easily present them to the whole class afterwards. This open and flexible learning environment supported effective flipping in the classroom, by allowing comfortable group work and movement in a classroom without physical boundaries and limitations of a traditional classroom.[38]

**Step 6:** The *Flipped Classroom* does not end with the students physically leaving the group space of the classroom. The teacher has to make sure that the students really reached the learning objectives and support them reinforcing the learned topic. This can be done by giving them some home assignment linked to the in-class activities, for instance in form of a clarification or summary of the in-class discussion. Or the students could be given some further reading connected with some more advanced questions which they should discuss online with each other on the university's learning platform's discussion board.

**Step 7:** The last step on the way to a successful implementation of the *Flipped Classroom* concept is the evaluation of the class. Now it is on the teacher to reflect upon the success of his or her design and implementation of flipping this specific class. Was the topic suitable for flipping? Was the provided pre-class video or audio introduction meaningful? Did the additional material sufficiently supplement the pre-class preparation? Were both video/audio and the additional material able and effective to trigger students' motivation for self-learning before class? Did students use the opportunity to get in touch with the teacher before class? What kind of questions or comments did they have? How well prepared did the students arrive in class? How was the students' feedback for the pre-class instruction? What did the short review activity at the beginning of the class show about the students' level of remembering and understanding the concepts being presented in the pre-class video or audio? Were the chosen learning activities in-class suitable for the students to apply, analyse and evaluate the most relevant parts of the lesson's topic? Did all students actively participate in the in-class activities? Was there any need for additional explana-

---

38 Şahin / Fell Kurban, *The New University Model*, pp. 219.

tions or motivation for the students? Which positive and negative outcomes did the teacher observe during the group work? How was the students' feedback related to the in-class activities? Did the performance of the in-class activities correspond with the teacher's set expectations? Did the students still take the opportunity to reinforce their knowledge about the lesson's topic in the after-class assignments? What kind of questions and problems still occurred after class? Could the previously set learning outcomes be reached at the end? Was it worth flipping the classroom for this specific topic? What could be done better in case of repeating the same lesson in flipped style?

These are just some examples of questions which the teacher could ask him or herself in evaluating the given class in the style of the *Flipped Classroom*. Especially for beginners, it cannot be expected that the entire concept of flipping a class turned out to be a big success. It is mostly a matter of trial and error. This helps each teacher to improve. As for everyone, it also applies for the teachers: We learn from our mistakes to make it better next time. However, the teachers should not only focus on the things which did not go well, they should also be aware of the strong parts of their performance and build on them for the future classes.

## C. What are the Pros and Cons of the Flipped Classroom?

As for every type of educational strategy or teaching and learning approach, the *Flipped Classroom* has its strong and weak points. These all need to be considered before making a decision to flip a class or even a whole course. Let's start with the arguments which might keep you away from flipping your classroom:

First of all, switching from traditional teaching to a *Flipped Classroom* teaching requires motivated students and relies on preparation and trust. As nearly all students are only used to the traditional methods of teaching and learning, they might be sceptical about turning the common learning habits upside down. To do the inevitable preparation work prior to class on their own, the students need to be sufficiently motivated. In order to feel motivated, the prominent *Self-Determination Theory* argues that there are three basic psychological needs that should be fulfilled: need for competence, need for autonomy and need for relatedness. The need for competence refers to the feeling of having the ability to complete a task. The need for autonomy refers to the feeling of volition when performing a task. The need for relatedness refers to a sense of belonging and support from a social group.[39] Studies have shown that fulling these three needs would promote students' motivation to learn.[40] The crucial point for motivating the students to do their pre-class work is to give them the feeling that they are able to complete the task and that it will be beneficial for them in class, for understanding the topic and for being well prepared for the exam.

Another disadvantage of the *Flipped Classroom* that might be connected with missing student motivation is that this form of active learning, which lays its focus on the learning process, is not naturally a test-preparation form of learning. This is what we found out practising the *Flipped Classroom* for the first years at MEF University: When students were asked why they did not engage with the pre-class videos and why they did not participate as expected in class, they answered that their main concern was passing the final exam at the end of the course and not the regular participation in class.[41] So, if the students' assessment is still held the traditional way with written midterm and final exams, only flipping the instruction but not the form of assessment gives the students the signal that the value of learning is still in the final exam, not in the learning process.

Implementing the *Flipped Classroom* concept in a proper way needs technical equipment and devices. This might be an obstacle for some universities that are (financially) not able or willing to provide the necessary equipment at the university facilities. In addition to that, also the teachers and each student need to be equipped at home with at least a computer, laptop, tablet or smartphone and, of course, stable internet access. This might make it impossible for some students to participate in the *Flipped Classroom* activities as needed. But it might also deter a teacher from flipping a class when he or she is not familiar with recording pre-class video or audio introductions and uploading them onto the university's learning platform.

A downside for the teacher is that he or she has to conduct significant work prior to class. It takes much more time to design, prepare and implement a *Flipped Classroom* lesson than a lesson being performed in the traditional style.

Also, during the whole process of implementing the *Flipped Classroom*, the teacher needs much more time for monitoring than in traditional

---

39 Vallerand, Robert G. / Ratelle, Catherine F., *Intrinsic and Extrinsic Motivation: A Hierarchical Model*, in: Deci, Edward L. / Ryan, Richard M. (Eds.), *Handbook of self-determination research*, Rochester 2002, pp. 48.

40 Abeysekera, Lakmal / Phillip Dawson, *Motivation and cognitive load in the flipped classroom: definition, rationale and a call for research*, in: Higher Education Research & Development 34.1 (2015), pp. 1–14.

41 Şahin / Fell Kurban, *The New University Model*, p. 62.

classroom settings. The idea of the *Flipped Classroom* is based on fostering active learning, and this can only be successful when the students get sufficient guidance and monitoring during the phases of active learning.

To enjoy the full benefit from the *Flipped Classroom* approach, the flipped learning philosophy has to be embedded through all three channels of effective learning: curriculum, instruction and assessment.[42] Especially, in the Law faculties this is an extremely difficult task, as the curricula and assessments are mostly not within the decision-making authority and the scope or discretion of each university. In particular, as long as the assessment of Law students still only focuses on formal exams, not on the learning process, the possible benefits of the *Flipped Classroom* method will be diminished, because the students lack in being honoured for their performance and progress during the learning process.

In contrast to these drawbacks, the *Flipped Classroom* approach also offers some significant advantages:

First of all, implementing the *Flipped Classroom* results in better prepared students in class. Thanks to the pre-class instructions by video/audio and additional material, the students already arrive in class with at least some pre-knowledge about the topic. This enables the teacher to provide more in-depth guidance on the topic inside the classroom by practising active learning with the students.

A big advantage of the *Flipped Classroom* method for the students is that they have more control of the whole learning process. They can access and watch the pre-class videos/audios and additional material that is provided online anytime and anywhere and as often as they want or need. This offers the students the possibility to learn at their own space, according to their own technique, their own speed and in their preferred learning environment. The lessons' content is more and easier accessible as before.

Closely connected with this advantage is the benefit that students who are not able to attend a certain lesson for some reasons such as illness, are easily able to catch up on the missed lesson by accessing the pre-class and after-class material online and work through the lesson's content on their own. In case of any questions, they can also easily contact their classmates or the teacher and ask for help or assistance.

Beyond that, the *Flipped Classroom* promotes student-centred learning and collaboration. During the class hours, the students engage in various hands-on activities that facilitate deeper learning, practice and mastery of concepts. The teachers can plan for discussions, peer reviews and different

---

42 Şahin / Fell Kurban, *The New University Model*, p. XXVI.

project-based learning activities to strengthen learning and facilitate collaboration between students. In addition, the *Flipped Classroom* also enhances collaboration between the students and the teacher as the teacher can intervene in the group work anytime to assist, correct or clarify during the learning process.

The use of supportive technical equipment such as the tools of the university's learning platform as well as the regular processing of formative assessments such as quizzes, summaries, responses and other methods of checking the students' comprehension and completion of the required learning tasks also offers the teacher the collection of meaningful formative data in the *Flipped Classroom*. This can be used to assess the performance of the students and to evaluate the success of each *Flipped Classroom* session and the whole flipped course. The collected data serves as a valuable source of a regular in-class evaluation.

Finally, once prepared, the implementation of a *Flipped Classroom* lesson takes less time when holding it for a second or third time. The time-consuming preparation of the pre-class video/audio and the design of the in-class activities falls away. The teacher can build his or her own database of pre-class videos and audios that can be reused. If desired, the teacher can even share these pre-recorded videos and audios with colleagues and edit them based on the feedback received.

## D. Conclusion

The *Flipped Classroom* approach is a very promising and effective method of teaching and learning. However, its success mainly depends on the teacher's openness for innovation and the students' motivation to conscientiously and continuously work on their own at home. This responsibility of the students should be expected at University. Therefore, provided with a suitable learning environment, the *Flipped Classroom* method also provides great opportunities for Law classes. Relocating much of the theoretical background from the traditional lecture to the pre-class space, there would be more time in class to get deeper into the subject and to apply, analyse and evaluate legal problems together with the students in the classroom. This would be an effective way of better preparing the students for their future professions as in the legal business critical thinking, analytical and argumentative skills as being taught in the *Flipped Classroom* are of high practical relevance.

# The Teaching of Legal Practice in Europe: An Outlook

*Maria Meng-Papantoni*[*]

I would like, first, to thank the members of the ELPIS-Conference[1] and especially Prof. Dr. Germelmann for the honour of inviting me to take part in this event and to discuss with you the issues surrounding European legal studies – the current status of the discipline, how we can strengthen this teaching, and the outlook for the field – all of which concern the audience here, teachers and students alike.

In today's discussion[2] we have traced the current state of affairs and how we could enhance more generally the teaching of legal practice through study programmes[3], and technical and human support, and the kind of

---

[*] Prof. Dr. Maria Meng-Papantoni, Associate Professor of European Business Law, Panteion University, Athens (Greece) and Director of the European Center of Economic and Financial Law of the Panteion University. She also is Visiting Lecturer at the Europa-Institut at Saarland University. This article is based on a presentation held on occasion of a Conference of the ELPIS Network Meeting in Hannover on 14 December 2019. The lecture style has been maintained; some footnotes have been added.

[1] From 12 December 2019 to 14 December 2019 the ELPIS Network Meeting was organized by the Faculty of Law of the Leibniz Universität Hannover. The meeting was concluded by a conference, which was devoted to the topic of innovative teaching in European legal education.

[2] On 14 December 2019, the third day of the meeting, the conference "Innovative Teaching in European Legal Education" took place. It was opened by the Dean of the Faculty of Law of the Leibniz Universität Hannover, Prof. Dr. Dr. h.c. Bernd H. Oppermann, LL.M., Prof. h.c. and the Dean of Studies of the same Faculty Prof. Dr. Claas Friedrich Germelmann, LL.M., who addressed the participants with their welcoming speeches, underlining the important place that innovative teaching methods have at the Member Universities.

[3] The law curriculum remains largely insulated from major societal transformations, such as the democratization of knowledge through technological development or the disruptive effects brought about by the sharing-economy. Susan McClellan, *Externships for Millennial Generation Law Students: Bridging the Generation Gap*, 15 CLINICAL L. REV. 255 (2009). https://digitalcommons.law.seattleu.edu/faculty/157.

teaching of European law that we want and are able to provide[4]. And I think that we have managed to produce a number of useful conclusions on which to build.

One observation that came to my mind at the outset of our proceedings concerns the ambiguity contained in the title of the conference. Given that the conference aims to explore the "Teaching of legal practice in Europe", we need to ask "What is the teaching of legal practice?" Does it only concern European law[5], or is it the teaching in general of law, as taught in the law schools of the various European states? And do these states include the states of the European continent[6] or only the member-states of the European Union[7]? These questions need to be borne in mind, as they concern the discussion regarding the geographical limits of the EU as well as current developments following the outcome of the last elections in the UK[8]. In light of the presentations that we have seen here, and the content of our

---

4　The European legal teaching -historically formalistic, doctrinal, hierarchical and passive (lecture and text-book based) – is coming under increasing pressure to reimagine itself as pragmatic, policy-aware and action-oriented. Alberto Alemanno & Lamin Khadar, *Reinventing Legal Education: How Clinical Education Is Reforming the Teaching and Practice of Law in Europe*. Cambridge: Cambridge University Press (2018) HEC Paris Research Paper No. LAW-2018–1293. Available at SSRN: https://ssrn.com/abstract=3185959.

5　Definition of European Law according to Encyclopaedia Britannica: "European law, laws and legal traditions that are either shared by/ or characteristic of the countries of Europe. Broadly speaking, European law can refer to the historical, institutional, and intellectual elements that European legal systems tend to have in common; in this sense it is more or less equivalent to Western law. More commonly and more specifically, however, European law refers to the supranational law, especially of the European Union, that unites most of the national legal systems within Europe". Carozza, P. (2015, November 22). *European law* [Retrieved 10.03.2020, from https://www.britannica.com/topic/European-law].

6　There are 44 countries in Europe today, according to the United Nations.

7　The Union currently counts 27 EU countries. The United Kingdom withdrew from the European Union on 31 January 2020. European Union. 2020. Countries | European Union. [online] Available at: <https://europa.eu/european-union/about-eu/countries_en> [Accessed 10.03.2020].

8　Prime Minister Boris Johnson and his Conservative Party secured a landslide victory in the British general election that took place in 2019: McCann, A., Leatherby, L., & Migliozzi, B. (2019, December 13), U.K. Election Results Map: How Conservatives Won in a Landslide. The New York Times. Retrieved from https://www.nytimes.com/interactive/2019/12/13/world/europe/uk-general-election-results.html
The UK formally left the EU on 31 January 2020, but there is still a lot to talk about and months of negotiation to come. This will need to be worked out during the transition period, which began immediately after Brexit day and is due to end on 31 December 2020. During this 11-month period, the UK will continue to

discussions, it appears that European teaching of legal practice is the teaching which covers the totality of legal studies of those countries that decided to participate in the united European project. This is the approach that my own presentation regarding the outlook for the European teaching of legal practice takes its starting point.

So what is the outlook for the European teaching of legal practice? I believe that it is rich and exciting – it concerns both the human resources that comprise it, including especially the students to whom we turn on the basis of their academic background, and, secondly, the geographical reach of our discipline.

Regarding the first of these points, i.e. our target students: In recent years we hear more and more, from both scientists and the heads of major corporations, about the massive changes that are going to take place above all in the workplace as a result of the ongoing technological revolution in artificial intelligence[9]. Even if we only have a hazy idea of the exact nature of these changes, it is almost certain that the times ahead will cause upheaval in substantial areas of working life, even in what may have seemed unshakeable professional fields such as the legal profession[10]. The career prospects of our future students will most likely require a combination of

---

follow all of the EU's rules and its trading relationship will remain the same. The transition period is meant to give both sides some breathing space while a new free trade agreement is negotiated.

9 The term 'Artificial Intelligence' (AI) can be applied to computer systems which are intended to replicate human cognitive functions. In particular, it includes 'machine learning', where algorithms detect patterns in data, and apply these new patterns to automate certain tasks. Artificial Intelligence and the Legal Profession. (n.d.). *The Law Society* [Retrieved 15.03.2020, from https://www.academia.edu/369 20594/Artificial_Intelligence_and_the_Legal_Profession].

10 Lawyers are already using AI to do things like reviewing documents during litigation and due diligence, analyzing contracts to determine whether they meet predetermined criteria, performing legal research, and predicting case outcomes. Within a few years, AI will be taking over (or at least affecting) a significant amount of work now done by lawyers. Thirty-nine percent of in-house counsel expect that AI will be commonplace in legal work within ten years. On a more philosophical level, lawyers should understand that the "decisions" made by AI-powered software will raise significant legal questions, including those of tort liability and of criminal guilt. For example, if AI is controlling a driverless car and someone's killed in an accident, who's at fault? A Primer on Using Artificial Intelligence in the Legal Profession. (n.d.). *Harvard Journal of Law & Technology* [Retrieved 15.03.2020, from https://jolt.law.harvard.edu/digest/a-primer-on-using-artificial-intelligence-in-the-legal-profession].

many areas of knowledge[11]. I therefore believe that this will be one of the key objectives of the teaching of law in Europe, which for the most part has stayed somewhat stuck to the idea of segmentation of the various branches of the discipline, as it developed in the era after the first industrial revolution.

The teaching of law in Europe will naturally continue to concern the strictly legal profession, but in my view it will need to prepare for an ever-increasing interaction with the schools of other disciplines[12]. This is already happening to some extent, since certain branches of law are being

---

11 Lawyers of the future must match a deep understanding of the law with a host of other technical knowledge and soft skills to remain competitive. This is the so-called lawyer 2.0. The term was developed to demonstrate the changing skill set of the future lawyer. The skills and competencies previously required by lawyers when embarking on their careers are no longer the same. The next generation of lawyers should acquire the following set of skills: strong legal expertise and at the same time an appreciation and understanding of other disciplines including technology, business, analytics, and data security. Lawyers must remain up-to-date on changes in regulation and case law, apply critical thinking to evaluate how this may impact upon their client, and creatively consider the appropriate advice and best possible solution to offer. In that sense, lawyers should not lose focus on the core competencies the profession has always been known for, and see technology as a way to further expand their skill set. See more at IE Law School. (2019, October 28). The skills, tools and knowledge every future lawyer needs [Retrieved 15.03.2020, from https://www.ie.edu/law-school/news-events/news/skills-tools-kno wledge-every-future-lawyer-needs/].

12 Law affects and is affected by other disciplines and other professions in at least three ways. First, some other area of knowledge and the disciplines and practices which concern it may at times be the subject of legal control and regulation: for example, legal regulation significantly affects the promulgation of knowledge and expertise in the liberal arts, through constraints on a university's system of promotion and tenure. Second, the expertise provided by another organized body of knowledge may at times be necessary to the resolution of a particular legal issue. The "expert testimony" of a mental health professional, for example, is often central to a judgment of culpability or non-culpability in a criminal law proceeding. And third, law may be the subject matter of another discipline. Thus, the study of law might be sensibly regarded as not only preparation for a profession, but also as a branch of the humanities or the social sciences. If so, then literature, philosophy, cultural studies, economics, history, or sociology might all provide insights into the nature of law.
Georgetown University Law Center. (n.d.). *Law and Other Disciplines.* [Retrieved 16.03.2020, from https://curriculum.law.georgetown.edu/jd/law-other-disciplines /].

taught, for instance, in engineering faculties[13], in schools focusing on economics, and so on. I feel that soon this should be done in a more systematic way so that the teaching of our own field, and its various component courses, does not become an outcast within a pool of courses that relate to other academic disciplines.

We will need to develop other kinds of collaboration so that our courses are more outward-looking. For instance, here in Germany a case in point is the studies programme of the winter semester in the School of Engineering of the well-known University of Aachen. Under the syllabus that is comprised of engineering courses, there is also one course on private law[14]. This amounts to noteworthy and tangible recognition of our specific field of knowledge, but surely – given the developments that are rapidly evolving – it would be a good idea if all university professors together define the new mode of teaching. And one thing that is certain, is that the teaching of legal practice is not going to be side-lined, since as we start to deal with the new, emerging situation, new rules on how this situation is incorporated into our lives – including new labour relations and new business relations – will emerge too[15].

---

13 Learning law which is relevant to the engineers does not only provide students with an opportunity to take a peek into another world and to try out their hand at another discipline but it provides them with a knowledge of the legal framework in an engineering environment. Such knowledge is useful whether they remain in the profession or not. Should the engineers decide to become lawyers, their 'technological perspectives' will be useful in understanding law grounded in an engineering context like construction law. Ng, J. (1997). *Should Law Be Introduced into the Engineering Curriculum?* International Journal of Engineering Education, 13(1), 72–78 [Retrieved 16.03.2020, from https://www.ijee.ie/contents/c1 30197.html].

14 According to the syllabus of Civil Engineering M.Sc. "The four-semester Master's program in civil engineering will prepare you for the complex demands of challenging construction, planning and infrastructure projects. With its eight program concentrations you can expand your expertise in many areas of civil engineering. The Master's program promotes independent work and teaches methods of scientific problem solving. You learn to develop, plan and realize technical projects as a whole and with a view to economical, ecological and legal aspects."

15 For instance, a report of The Law Society of New South Wales sheds light on the changes that are taking place within our profession. Some of their findings include that: 1) Artificial intelligence raises regulatory and ethical issues that require investigation and guidance for solicitors, 2) There is an urgent need for funding for legal assistance and a role for technology and innovation to aid access to justice, 3) The law graduate of the future needs a range of new skills and knowledge, 4) New areas of work and new roles are likely to emerge with technology, 5) New ways of working are proliferating and 6) Connectivity and globalisation raise new

Such, then, is the need for our teaching to open up – particularly since we shall probably have no choice! – when we see that a computer programme will be far cheaper than the human intervention of a lawyer, that it will be able to solve a host of legal issues that today provide lawyers with plenty of work. I believe that everything we have discussed today regarding the latest teaching methods and syllabuses will be of value, and provide significant support, in preparing to work alongside other academic disciplines.

Now, a few words about the geographical reach of European teaching of legal practice:

We should not forget that we have the comparative advantage of the internal market[16], which, given that it generates law and economic power, means that this law has to be understood and followed – even if the teaching of legal practice in Europe is first and foremost aimed at, and concerns, students from countries that are within the European internal market.

On a second level, the teaching of law in Europe is undoubtedly a pole of attraction for students from outside Europe[17]. I can say this from personal experience, as – I am sure – can most other people in this room.

---

and great opportunities and threats for lawyers. Globalisation is challenging domestic law reform. See more at The Law Society of New South Wales. (2017). *The Future of Law and Innovation in the Profession (The Flip report)* (pp. 4–5) [Retrieved 17.03.2020, from https://www.lawsociety.com.au/sites/default/files/2018-03/12729 52.pdf].

16 The single/internal market refers to the EU as one territory without any internal borders or other regulatory obstacles to the free movement of goods, people and services. A functioning single market stimulates competition and trade, improves efficiency, raises quality, and helps cut prices. The European single market is one of the EU's greatest achievements. It has fueled economic growth and made the everyday life of European businesses and consumers easier. See the definition and more at European Commission. (2017, July 5), *The European single market* [Retrieved 17.03.2020, from https://ec.europa.eu/growth/single-market_en].

17 In 2017, over 460 000 first residence permits for third-country nationals were issued for study reasons in the EU. The highest number of international students in the EU came from China, which made up almost a quarter of all first study permits issued to international students in 2017 (118 830 permits). Regarding the popularity of different study fields among international students, business administration and law seemed to be the most attractive across the majority of Member States. See more information at European Migration Network (2019). Attracting and Retaining International Students in the EU. Brussels: European Migration Network. Retrieved 17.03.2020, from https://ec.europa.eu/homeaffairs/sites/home affairs/files/00_eu_international_students_2018_synthesis_report.pdf].

And then we also see the penetration of European teaching of legal practice into courses run at universities outside the EU[18], a phenomenon that could potentially impact exponentially on strengthening the previous point we just considered. But I think this is a point which – without wishing to presume anything he might have to say – Professor Hugg, our eminent colleague from the States[19], is better placed to discuss in more detail and share with us his views and experience.

To close, I would like to stress the comparative advantage that European legal studies can boast. The teaching of European law is not confined to the traditional areas – i.e. institutional law, law of the internal market, and competition law – but today covers law in all its branches[20]. This is the lingua franca of legal science today in the member states of the EU. After more than 60 years since the establishment of the single European project it is clear that we need to embrace and harness its advantages. Given the fact that the European Union is a major global economic and commercial power[21], knowledge of its legal structures and methods automatically gives students of its law, both living within its territories and outside, particular added value.[22]

---

18 A distinctive example is Harvard Law School, which has a whole course dedicated to the European law. For more information, see the university's official website. Harvard Law School. (2014). Course Catalog: European Union Law [Retrieved 17.03.2020, from https://hls.harvard.edu/academics/curriculum/catalog/index.htm l?o=67711].

19 Professor Hugg took part in the 5th Panel of the ELPIS Conference presenting his own experience of the teaching of legal studies in the USA.

20 In other words, the EU can pass laws concerning areas like: the environment, energy, space etc. See all the areas of EU action at European Commission (2019, October 10). Areas of EU action [Retrieved 17.03.2020, from https://ec.europa.eu/inf o/about-european-commission/what-european-commission-does/law/areas-eu-acti on_en].

21 Europe today is a genuine superpower and will likely remain one for decades to come. By most objective measures, it either rivals or surpasses the United States and China in its ability to project a full spectrum of global military, economic, and soft power. Europe consistently deploys military troops within and beyond its immediate neighbourhood. It manipulates economic power with a skill and success unmatched by any other country or region. And its ability to employ "soft power" to persuade other countries to change their behaviour is unique. See Moravcsik, A. (2017, April 13). *Europe Is Still a Superpower.* Foreign Policy [Retrieved 17.03.2020, from https://foreignpolicy.com/2017/04/13/europe-is-still-a-sup erpower/].

22 An interesting article in the Guardian encourages UK law students to get to grips with the EU law as it will boost their careers because EU law is essential in their lives, something that many people ignore. See more at MacQueen, F. (2014, April

We need only think of what happened in recent years. Prior to the financial crisis, more often than not, young legal professionals studied the law of the other member states of the EU in the context of their postgraduate studies. They did this usually in order to expand their knowledge and to better acquaint themselves with another legal system that might help them later find work in their home country more easily. This general set-up has changed significantly, at least in the case of those countries – by no means few – that were particularly hard hit by the crisis.

The economic crisis resulted – among other things – in many talented and qualified young people leaving their home countries: what is commonly termed the 'brain drain'. The crisis showed us, in the bluntest of terms, the arrival in the European Union of a phenomenon that we have seen for decades in the US – i.e. the movement of the dynamic part of the workforce from one part of the internal market to another in order to find work and make a living. Problems relating to language or the singularities of a member state's legal system may in the past have proved to be obstacles to the easy movement of people in the legal profession from one country to another; yet in the years of the economic crisis they did not prevent law professionals, with qualifications from other member states, from taking up jobs and making their lives elsewhere within the single market. In other words, throughout these difficult years we have seen young law professionals, equipped with a knowledge of European law, deepening their legal expertise in other countries of the EU beyond their home country, and thereby successfully joining the legal profession or taking part more generally in the provision of legal and related services in their adopted countries[23].

---

29). *What's the point of studying EU law?* The Guardian [Retrieved 17.03.2020, from https://www.theguardian.com/law/2014/apr/29/whats-the-point-studying-la w].

23 Lawyers take up a unique position when it comes to the legal regime for free movement applicable to them in the European Union. Since the consolidation of the directives applicable to the medical professions and architects in Directive 2005/36/EC, the profession of lawyer is the only (liberal) profession that is covered by a separate system of Directives: the Lawyers' Services Directive (77/249/ EEC) and the Lawyers' Establishment Directive (98/5/EC). The system applicable to lawyers specifically employs a unique mechanism of mutual recognition, without (immediate) integration into the profession of the receiving Member State. Besides the two Lawyers' Directives, lawyers can also make use of the general system of Directive 2005/36, which leads to full integration in the profession of the receiving Member State. Under this regime, to proceed to full integration, a lawyer must first successfully complete an aptitude test. The Lawyers' Establish-

It would argue that for the European project to succeed, it is essential that this potential for younger professionals, across the whole range of specializations, to move freely within the single market in order to exercise their profession is strengthened and encouraged. This can be done by providing bright young people aiming to enter the legal and other professions with a solid background in law, so that they will be able to deal with issues regarding the national law of the various EU member states. And I believe that today's endeavours to identify and formulate uniform teaching programmes for legal studies is leading in this direction[24]. Ultimately we shall be able to achieve a significant degree of uniformity across the Union in the exercise and provision of legal services, while students will automatically be qualified to work anywhere throughout the Union, overcoming the barriers that once existed due to the divergences in the various national legal systems[25].

---

ment Directive also offers a possibility to integrate fully in the legal profession, without the need to do an aptitude test, but only after the lawyer in question has practiced for three years in the receiving country under the system of the Lawyers' Establishment Directive. See Evaluation of the Legal Framework for the Free Movement of Lawyers Final Report Project number: BA03973 This study has been financed by the European Commission, DG Internal Market and Services (MARKT/2011/071/E) Mr. Dr. S.J.F.J. Claessens, M.C.C. van Haeften MSc, Dr. N.J. Philipsen, Drs. B.J. Buiskool, prof. dr. H.E.G.S. Schneider, Dr. S.L.T. Schoenmaekers, drs. D.H. Grijpstra, prof. dr. H.J. Hellwig (advisor). Zoetermeer, November 28, 2012 [Retrieved 17.03.2020, from https://docplayer.net/2981876-Evaluation-of-the-legal-framework-for-the-free-movement-of-lawyers.html].

24 A very interesting initiative towards this direction is that of the European Commission which wants to construct a common European Education Area. See https://ec.europa.eu/education/education-in-the-eu/european-education-area_en.
Also universities have reacted to these European initiatives by creating new courses and programmes responding to the European integration and globalisation… they have included courses on international and European law in the basic law curriculum, often as a mandatory component of it. See Arzoz, X. (Ed.). (2012). *Bilingual Higher Education in the Legal Context: Group Rights, State Policies and Globalisation Studies in International Minority and Group Rights*. Martinus Nijhoff Publishers.p. 316–320.

25 The Europeanisation of law, legal scholarships, legal practice and legal culture must inevitably have an impact on legal education. This has two dimensions: The Europeanisation of higher education systems and a reorientation of the law curriculum towards a more European-oriented law curriculum. Ibid., p. 316.
In the words of Prof. Heringa, "In Europe we have to move towards another legal education; maybe not to a full-fledged reform of all European law schools, but at least to the establishment of Law Schools which cater specifically to the needs of European, transnational and international lawyers… There is one thing I am very sure of: reforming European legal training is absolutely necessary to ensure a

body of European lawyers to keep up with the intricacies and complexities of European and international law. Academia has to respond to that need, specifically when doing so promotes and ensures a top quality academic and intellectually stimulating education. Instead of legal education in Europe we can work towards European legal education." See the contribution of Heringa, A.-W. (2011). *European Legal Education or Legal Education in Europe.* Maastricht Journal of European and Comparative Law, 18, 222–224. doi: 10.1177/1023263X1101800301.

# Perspectives from the United States: Pioneering in Legal Education as Innovation Advances

*Patrick R. Hugg**

Note:

*The onset of the 2020 coronavirus pandemic has radically altered percep-tions about effective teaching techniques in legal education. Virtually overnight, thousands of legal educators and their students worldwide had been locked out of their university facilities, and forced forward into virtual classrooms, for better or worse. Most legal educators acknowledge that the technological, electronic revolution in education has been thrust upon us.*

*This article depicts the author's perceptions about legal education **pre-pan-demic**, as articulated in the author's presentation at the ELPIS conference in Hannover, Germany, on December 14, 2019. Unavoidably, this iteration of the author's views on legal education also includes reflections from the present experiences of the pandemic.*

*Preface*

The classroom may never be the same.

Rephrasing the existential issue for academics in 2020 becomes fearful. How will higher education go forward? And as it rapidly advances into new territories of socially-distanced learning, how effectively will we pro-fessors take advantage of advanced technologies and innovative teaching-learning research and experience, amid changed medical, social, and legal parameters? What is our brave, new world?

---

\* Prof. Dr. Patrick R. Hugg, Professor of Law Emeritus at the Loyola University Col-lege of Law, New Orleans, Louisiana (USA).

*Introduction*

The ambition of my presentation at this ELPIS Conference on Innovative Teaching in Legal Education in Hannover, Germany on December 14, 2019, was to develop more thoroughly my exploration on quality law teaching that I delivered at the preceding ELPIS Conference in Recife, Brazil, in June of 2019. My goal in Recife had been to probe ways for legal educators to more effectively generate student learning than was characteristic using our traditional, often criticized, lecture method. In this presentation today, I propose for consideration further highly innovative and dynamic teaching techniques that can generate student learning. The coronavirus pandemic radically impacts my (and other professors') recommendations discussed herein so long as and insofar as students are prohibited from working together in classes and small groups. Regardless, this discussion has value for times when such interaction is possible again, and more generally as it identifies ways to spark learning and more effectively teach.

This remains my central issue: How do academics today use innovative teaching techniques to engender learning? No longer a choice for most, the question becomes: how well we will adapt. We must ask: Can we teach more effectively? Can "virtual teaching" be a step forward? Are we, at last, unlocking old forms cast by tradition, trepidation, and bureaucracy? These are heady days.

*A.*

For most academics, our professional mission is threefold, as we seek to serve our students, our universities, and advance scientific research and analysis in our fields of expertise. Specifically, we are tasked with, first, teaching and leading our students effectively in their journeys towards to higher levels of understanding; second, researching and advancing inquiry into academic subjects; and third, engaging in university and community service.[1]

---

1 See Mary Kay Kane, *The Requirements of Full Time Faculty in American Legal Education: Responsibilities and Expectations*, 51 J. LEGAL EDUC. 372, 372 (2001)(quoting American Bar Association Standard 402(c) "A full time faculty member is one who during the academic year devotes substantially all working time to teaching and scholarship, participates in Law school governance and service,... and whose outside professional activities... are of service to the legal profession and the public generally....").

In my experience, the latter two of these tasks are not so difficult, at least at the basic level.[2] Many of us so enjoy our research and writing, peacefully cushioned in our libraries and offices, that this task can seem a pleasure.[3] In a different way, participating on university committees can be important, sometimes very important, but also often tedious and not so challenging. Community service collaborations can be personally and socially rewarding – enjoyable service to be sure. It is my submission that the more difficult challenge for many conscientious academics is the actual, effective teaching of students.[4]

In this endeavor, many of us struggle to motivate and generate learning, as our aspirations would lead us. We search for productive techniques to accomplish this. Recognizing that we cannot learn **for** them, we strive to motivate them to engage with the concepts and questions we pose, and we attempt to lure them up a figurative ladder to achieve thinking and learning at a fresh, creative, and incisive level.

We acknowledge that the students are the principal actors in this dramatic quest. If we read to them, we do little, and they do less. If we simply tell them to read, and then we test them, we may achieve the goal of forced, rote learning, but we teachers have done little to drive or engage their thinking capacity onward. How can we act effectively as protagonists in their intellectual journeys?

In my thirty-three years of teaching law students, one truth (at least) about the current state of U.S. law school instruction has been clear: While university law professors are expected to be experts and explorers in their chosen fields, they have traditionally focused less on pedagogy than on their scholarship. Many of us have embraced the teaching styles of those professors who delighted or frightened us when we were law students ourselves. And most professors can hardly resist the system in which they so excelled. So we tended to follow the traditional styles of our predecessors. Now we are forced to look forward.

---

2  To be sure, significant advances in scholarship and leadership require a prodigious combination of intellect, insight, and diligence. However, much of this day-to-day work seems less arduous.

3  At least until the final deadline for submission is upon us. A wise mentor once advised writers: the scholarly paper is never truly finished; the deadline has simply arrived.

4  Some academics with whom I have experience would disagree strongly, insisting that their foremost vocation is to research and write doctrine. Some of them consider teaching students to be a distraction.

It seems to me that quality teaching requires thoughtfulness, focus, and energy. As much as we take pride in our successes, we are sometimes disappointed in what we see around us – sometimes sensing that there are sleepwalkers amongst us – students and faculty – overwhelmed by tradition, busy schedules, and sometimes inadvertence. So many professors do engage the students, but when we read the essays on the exams, we get a "reality check." We discover that some students are fully onboard and can write beautiful recitations and theoretical explorations, but unfortunately occasionally, we discover a measure of the students are free-riders, or worse, disgruntled customers. How do we better serve them, or is that beyond our scope?

Perhaps novel ideas and techniques can arouse them. I attempt to propose some vivid candidates in this presentation.

*B.*

As I contemplated my own instructional methods in my classroom, I began searching for answers. How do we professors teach? How do our students learn?

In the U.S., we employ a diverse array of teaching methods: from the lecture method, to the case method, and the problem method, to the most celebrated, fiery technique: the Socratic Method. In Recife, I recommended Socratic dialogue and discipline as productive because it forces students to engage intellectually before they come to class, intently studying the cases to be discussed in the coming class. Only then could the professor drive the class discussion to its sharp exposition of the law and policy intended. Students were motivated to be prepared to respond to the live (sometimes embarrassing, sometimes terrifying) dialogue in which they were to be questioned didactically to reason aloud – in front of their peers – through the logic or illogic of the facts and legal rules involved. In my experience, the student work before class was often more productive because of the anxiety that preceded the class. It seems this technique may not be the most constructive or efficient.

The Socratic Method has traditionally been the bedrock of legal education; both in the United States and throughout the international legal community.[5] In fact, "the Socratic Method is almost universally acknowl-

---

5 *See* Lowell Bautista, *The Socratic Method as a Pedagogical Method in Legal Education*, University of Wollongong Research Online, 1 (2014).

edged as the defining characteristic of the American legal education system."[6] However, employing the Socratic Method as the sole teaching method in a law school education system has come under scrutiny in recent years. Professor Robert D. Dinerstein, director of the law clinic at American University Washington College of Law offered valid criticism in 2011, suggesting that the Socratic Method had its place in 1L classrooms, where "it can lead to more active student engagement than alternatives like the lecture method."[7] He continued, however, to opine that the method loses its effectiveness in a student's second and third year of school because the method over-relies on excerpts of appellate cases, fosters "passivity on the part of those students not involved in the dialogue," and it privileges the "professor as the sage on the stage"[8] in what may not be the most constructive learning relationship.

In the U.S. professors use it less and less today. It is likely a good thing that this method has fallen out of favor, often insulting to and unpopular with adult law students. Today, the most effective techniques also actively provoke the students' minds, but in more positive and productive ways. Nonetheless, as will be seen below, we will return to the crucial element of students studying and preparing mentally **before** their classes, in more constructive methods, as other teaching strategies are discussed. Some dramatic new techniques replacing the lecture and Socratic dialogue methods, include live, real-client law clinics, experiential components in regular courses, real-time international collaborative courses, and various forms of team-based learning (TBL).[9]

## C.

Live law clinics may offer the paradigmatic model, in which students actually work with clients, in a form of team-law practice under the supervision of an established lawyer/law professor. The students personally experience what legal representation is:, they meet actual clients with real needs, confronting real dilemmas, fashioning persuasive legal arguments, and ap-

---

6  Ibid.
7  Robert D. Dinerstein, *There Are Limitations to the Socratic Method*, The N.Y. Times, Dec. 15, 2011, https://www.nytimes.com/roomfordebate/2011/12/15/rethinking-how-the-law-is-taught/there-are-limitations-to-the-socratic-method.
8  Ibid.
9  Bringing terms such as "real" and "experiential" into the teaching equation so dramatically differs from the traditional class discussions of old judicial decisions.

pearing in real courtrooms – with real consequences! It doesn't get much better than that. At my law school, the law clinic[10] is large and successful. The Clinic serves indigent clients who need help with immigration law, family law, criminal law, and other legal matters. The students are taught multiple aspects of lawyering, from interviewing clients, assessing cases, penetrating contradicting versions of the case, crafting arguments and defenses, writing motions, and sometimes ultimately going to trial. In this model of learning through representation, everyone gains: the students, the clients, the justice system, and the community. Learning by doing, in the supporting context of superlative guidance from professors, seems unparalleled as a teaching method. Unfortunately, this method has limits. Supervised student legal representation is more time-consuming that traditional course work, and law clinics are costly, as the student faculty ratio is at times unitary. Today's uncertain finances in higher education cast uncertainty on tomorrow's law clinics. So our exploration for models continues.

One of the most popular experiential learning techniques in the U.S. is the live Moot Court course, in which students are assigned fictitious clients in difficult legal situations, as their cases process through appeals. Students must assess a seemingly authentic trial record, formulate and assess issues for appeal, research the law, fashion strategy, write appellate briefs for a fictional court of appeals (or the U.S. Supreme Court), then appear in simulated courtrooms to deliver real-life adversarial appellate arguments, with opponents arguing the contrary sides, with rebuttal and live questions for judges in black robes sitting at lofty appellate benches, all arguments video-ed, and graded. This has proved effective and popular, but this method is also limited by its demanding requirements of manpower for staffing, physical space, and consumption of students' time.

Many professors use other, less intense forms of "experiential learning" in their traditional courses. For example, in my principal courses on International Trade and the Law of the European Union, I require my students to concretely "experience" aspects of the course, though at a modest level, in interpersonal exercises. For example, in both courses, each student is required to research and deliver a significant oral presentation (of typically 25–35 minute duration), with high-quality PowerPoint support, teaching fellow classmates the relevant, pressing issues in their chosen EU Members

---

10 Loyola University College of Law's Stuart H. Smith Center Law Clinic & Center for Social Justice is recognized as one of the leading law clinics in the U.S. Loyola's Clinic and Gillis Long Poverty Law Center are directed by Professor William Quigley, an internationally recognized leader in clinical legal education.

States or WTO Member countries. Subsequently in the course, every student is required to participate in a seventy-five minute live debate on central issues in the courses (for example, "What is the best future for global cooperation? How best to restore the WTO to productivity? or "What is the best model for future European cooperation?," and so on.). In the EU course, students also participate in an actual "political" campaign and election of class members, leading to the negotiation of a parliamentary form of "government" to represent the class. Another engaging tool that I use involves law school supporting technology: students are required at frequent stages through the courses to privately take and pass "quizzes" online (Blackboard, Canvas, or some other platform that facilitates testing) to demonstrate that they are mentally prepared to proceed to the next level of learning in the course. This works well in assuring that students are constructing knowledge on which to advance to further learning, and as will be explained below, this is an essential component of the Team-Based Learning strategy.

### D.

My "experiential learning" machinations pale in comparison to what some pioneering law professors are doing with the latest technology and international exchanges. "Will technology-based innovation enable dynamic teaching in the classroom?" seems trite following the C-19 pandemic. In this ELPIS presentation, I discussed live, interactive classes shared electronically across oceans among students of different cultures and legal systems. The value of such seems obvious.

I recited my "epiphany moment" a few years ago, as I was leading students across the picturesque park linking the Hagia Sophia and the Blue Mosque in Istanbul. For some years, our law school produced Field Studies to key locations and institutions of the European Union and to Rome, Athens, and Istanbul exploring "The Roots of the Civil Law."[11] In this instance, we had spent the first evening in Istanbul at a welcome dinner with students from our host Yeditepe University, and a cordial time was enjoyed by all. The students went out after the dinner to socialize further in local venues. They had gotten to know each other.

---

11 In New Orleans and Louisiana as a whole, we take pride in our status as a "mixed jurisdiction" in which the Civil Law is honored.

That morning as we walked in peripatetic exploration, one of our student leaders enthused to me: "Professor, these Muslim students are just like us!"

So there it was: a student gaining visceral understanding of a truly significant truth through personal discovery, from a situation designed by a legal educator. Voila, the purpose of the experiential learning Field Study. No lecture or video, just real-time, real-life human interaction. The understanding the students achieved was irreplaceable.

In a different form of international experiences, many U.S. law schools offer study abroad programs, and many of them thrust their students into direct contact with peers from other cultures and nationalities. These also in my opinion provide life-long lessons in our common humanity, in addition to technical knowledge of comparative legal systems. Unfortunately, like live law clinics, these international travel programs provoking situational experiential learning can be excessively expensive for participants.

Thankfully, some inspired law faculty have found a way around that cost of international travel and have organized similar experiences using technology. Notably, some faculty have developed simultaneous, synchronous, real-time international collaborative courses. For example, Professor Christopher Kelley of the University of Arkansas School of Law in Fayetteville has offered a transnational Rule of Law Colloquium course since 1995. Offered each spring semester, this two-credit course has students in Fayetteville and in Ukraine, mostly in Lviv and Kyiv. Imagine students interacting live over 5,574 miles and eight time zones apart!

In the Spring 2020 semester, for example, sixteen Arkansas students and over twenty-five Ukrainian students met simultaneously using Lifesize for the Cloud as their internet-based videoconferencing platform. The Arkansas students, who included a Russian and a Nigerian, were in a classroom designed for distance education and equipped with eight monitors, four microphones, and three cameras that were controlled by a technician in an adjoining room. The Ukrainian students were in different locations using their personal or work computers and webcams. A professor in the University of Arkansas's Rome Center co-taught the course, and guest speakers joined the class from various locations, including Washington, D.C. After each class, Professor Kelley sent all the students links to the class's recording. When the University of Arkansas closed in March because of Covid-19, the course continued with the Arkansas student joining the class from their residences in the same way in which the Ukrainian students participated.

To take full advantage of its transnational nature, the course's theme focused on each student by asking each student, "What does the rule of law mean to you?" The course's coverage included sessions on the rule of law in Ukraine, Russia, Italy, Kenya, and Sierra Leone. And the course was discussion-based. The readings and in-class videos were selected to prompt discussions about the rule of law's many contested meanings, the psychology of corruption and whistleblowing, and policy and legal instruments for fighting corruption, such as the U.S. Foreign Corrupt Practices Act. In addition to drawing from the assigned readings, the students told of their personal experiences. A particularly poignant experience was offered by a Ukrainian student whose brother was killed during Ukraine's Revolution of Dignity.

The students are graded on their class participation and an essay written during the two-week exam period, which was extended for the Ukrainian students. The students were permitted to write about what the rule of law means to them or any other rule-of-law-related topic. Professor Kelley encouraged creative formats and some students' essays were mock interviews, short plays, and commentary on the rule of law in Shakespeare's works.

A more detailed look at the history of the course and suggestions for creating and managing transnational courses can be found in Christopher R. Kelley & Nataliia Borozdina, Institutionalizing the U.S. Law School Classroom: Lessons Learned from Teaching Transnationally, 52 International Lawyer 131 (1992). The article also covers teaching International Commercial Arbitration transnationally. The International Lawyer is a peer-reviewed publication of the American Bar Association's Section of International Law.[12]

Similarly, Prof. Michael Losavio from the Univ. of Louisville, Kentucky law school in the U.S. is sharing with Perm State University in Russia a course on criminal procedure and civil rights – 5,428 miles apart and also many time zones apart! Prof. Losavio:

"Even though Perm is 10 hours ahead of us, the students don't mind (too much) that we meet at 5:30 a.m. to do our presentations for the Russians, and we make it a breakfast party, too!" "Students would volunteer to do their class presentations via Skype to law classes at Perm State, usually via PowerPoint, and posted questions. The Russian students would, in turn, do reciprocal presentations over Skype. "Some of my students admitted that it was the coolest thing they'd done in college. And their presentations for the Russians (I did remind them they were representing their country...) were often better than when I was their primary audience."

---

12 Special thanks to Prof. Christopher Kelley for editing these descriptions of his pioneering work.

Consider the learning and understanding bubbling spontaneously from such international, cross-cultural, and focused dialogue! Credit must go to these educators who work so diligently and creatively to stimulate learning in their students.

## E.

Other teaching techniques based on science are being tested in legal education.[13] One particularly dynamic technique has attracted considerable scholarship and attention. The recent Winter 2019 Journal of Legal Education featured two articles discussing "team-based learning" (TBL), a nontraditional teaching – learning strategy. Professor Jodi S. Balsam of the Brooklyn Law School contributed *Teaming Up to Learn in the Doctrinal Classroom*,[14] and Professor Melissa H. Weresh of Drake University Law School offered *Assessment, Collaboration, and Empowerment: Team-Based Learning*.[15] Both articles provide a surfeit of explanatory descriptions of this highly promising, action-packed teaching approach.

Many dimensions of the TBL theory and practice should appeal to law professors intent on engaging their students in more effective ways (the focus of this conference presentation). Both articles opened with references to an earlier, excellent 2012 exposition on the TBL concept written by two of their accomplished predecessors in this field: Professor Sophie M. Sparrow of the University of New Hampshire School of Law and Dean Margaret Sova McCabe of the University of Arkansas School of Law, entitled *Team Based Learning in Law*.[16] Their introduction to the concept is impressive:

"We believe that Team-Based Learning is an effective and *transformative* teaching strategy for law school courses, providing a sustainable and efficient way to teach important legal knowledge, skills, and values. We recommend that law professors consider learning more about and trying this approach if they seek to engage students in active and collaborative learn-

---

13  See, *e.g.*, Melissa H. Weresh, *Assessment, Collaboration, and Empowerment: Team Based Learning*, 68 J. Legal Educ. 303, 303 (2019)("Law schools, while historically slow to change, are increasingly turning to new teaching methodologies.).

14  Jodi S. Balsam, *Teaming Up to Learn in the Doctrinal Classroom*, 68 J. Legal Educ. 261 (2019).

15  Weresh, *supra* note 13, at 303.

16  Sophie M. Sparrow & Margaret Sova McCabe, *Team-Based Learning in Law*, 18 Legal Writing J. Legal Writing Inst. 153 (2012).

ing experiences, to have their students' learning be the center of attention in the classroom, and to help their students' learning improve."[17]

The authors offered their vision of Team-Based Learning, explaining reasons for adopting it, especially in view of recent criticisms of traditional legal education in the U.S., citing concrete examples of the teaching strategy in action, and discussing their use of and experiences with it over several years.

Professor Weresh adds: "The [TBL] method is particularly compelling in light of new accreditation standards requiring law schools to engage in assessment of student learning, new approaches to fostering professional identity development, and increasing need for law schools to foster collaboration and teamwork."[18]

In their seminal article, Professor Sparrow and Dean McCabe continue: "Team-Based Learning is a learner-centered teaching strategy designed to promote students' true understanding of a subject. [TBL] builds on the principles of effective teaching and learning research by engaging students in active and collaborative learning experiences throughout a course."[19] They explain their description of TBL as a "transformative" strategy further, as it combines such appealing elements of effective teaching as continuous "assessment and feedback, active and collaborative learning techniques, and student accountability," requiring students to "engage in high levels of thinking to solve complex problems."[20] Professor Balsam adds that students also praise TBL as productive and, as one student put it: "I loved the idea of building teams to participate in class.... It was a nice break from professors lecturing *AT* us."[21]

Sparrow and McCabe elaborate: "Used for over thirty years in a wide variety of fields, Team-Based Learning is a powerful teaching strategy that improves student learning. Used effectively, it enables students to actively engage in applying legal concepts in every class – without sacrificing coverage. Because this teaching strategy has been used in classes with over 200 students, it also provides an efficient and affordable way to provide significant learning. Based on the principles of instructional design, Team-Based

---

17  Sparrow & McCabe, *supra* note 16, at 154 (emphasis added.).
18  Weresh, *supra* note 13, at 304–305.
19  Sparrow & McCabe, *supra* note 16, at 156.
20  Ibid.
21  Jodi S. Balsam, *supra* note 14, at 261.

Learning has built-in student accountability, promotes independent student preparation, and fosters professional skills."[22]

Such promises! Intrigued readers may ask how such a bouquet of teaching blessings can be arranged. Note well that all of its advocates answer that TBL works only with proper design and diligent application, including certain mandatory elements, as are set forth below.

Sparrow and McCabe describe one of their typical TBL classes, in which eighty law students are teamed up in small groups of five to seven students, and then the groups are charged with assessing a common set of hypothetical facts and issues that represent the subject problem or issue to be solved, each related to a learning unit in the course's progression of topics.[23] The semester's work may comprise four to seven of these general topics covering the course syllabus plan.

The students in the groups set to work, "teaming up" to approach the challenge. They start with homework before the first group meeting, so that team members arrive armed with the topical information and ready to discuss basic issues fluently. Then in a dramatic design component, when they do arrive at the first class group meeting, the students are confronted with a test (or two) to insure their preparation. After the students' readiness has been assured, the groups discuss among themselves their views on the questions presented, their common assessment of the relevant facts and law, and they work together to agree on their decision-making strategy, ultimately yielding a conclusion.

At the end of the intra-groups' deliberation time period, each group is called upon to announce to the whole class its evaluation of the problem: in the authors' example, at the conclusion of the discussion period "all groups simultaneously hold up a sheet of paper identifying" the most significant facts in the issue or other aspect of their assessment of the better way to resolve the problem. The teacher moderates as the various groups attempt to publicly "justify their answer or argue against another group's response. The students are focused, engaged, and illustrate their points with the readings and previous class discussions. They focus on the person speaking, whether professor or classmate."[24]

After this intensely communal discussion, necessitating and involving the students' face-to-face appearances, the teacher gives brief feedback, syn-

---

22  Sparrow, *supra* note 16. (Quotation is from the Abstract of the Article available at https://papers.ssrn.com/sol3/papers.cfm?abstract_id=1986230.).
23  Sparrow & McCabe, *supra* note 16, at 153.
24  Ibid.

opsizing the group's contributions, and then offering a clarifying and synthesizing closing mini-lecture to reinforce primary principles.

In the following scheduled class, the same process is employed, using the next topic or issue, progressively advancing the problem-solving continuum of accumulated learning of the groups through the semester. This scenario portrays what students do throughout the semester, working "strategically and effectively in small groups for eighty percent of the class time."[25]

The authors argue convincingly that, using this human, action-packed technique, laden with natural public performance peer pressure, students learn more legal concepts and how to apply them than even in the authors' own best regular classes that combine lecture, Socratic dialogue, and active learning assignments.[26]

This seems to me to be a potentially radical improvement of traditional law classroom instruction – in the examples cited, the students' minds seem to be in gear, working, struggling, to reason out quality thinking. The authors continue:

"By the end of the semester, all students have repeatedly engaged in doing what lawyers do in practice: working together to solve significant problems. In doing so, the students learn how to interact professionally with others, build upon their group members' understanding of important doctrine, and learn from others' skills in communicating, solving problems creatively, studying, managing time, and resolving conflict. This is not a law school fantasy: this is Team-Based Learning in law school."[27]

To some, this may still sound like a fantasy, but in reality it can only be the result of arduous preparatory work by the professors. As one would expect, engineering such an active, fertile class requires considerable advance preparation by the professor, but then once the class is in session – in motion – the students are heavily and intimately engaged in problem-solving discussions: a momentous achievement for the virtuous teacher! The professor's teaching has moved from lecturing primarily, to stimulating the natural energies and talents of the students in action.

Design, Structure, and Process are fundamental to making this magic happen, all contributors seem to agree.[28] This is the arduous part for the course designer/professor, but it is existentially essential. These descrip-

---

25 Ibid. at 153.
26 Ibid. at 153–54.
27 Ibid. at 154.
28 See *e.g.*, Balsam, *supra* note 14, at 270–272. Copious resources to support TBL are available at Team-Based Learning Collaborative at www.teambasedlearning.org

tions might seem too good to be true, yet a closer look reveals that TBL is everything they say it is, and more: all of the authors stress that the professors who use TBL must dedicate considerable preparatory time and effort to make it work. "Introducing TBL in most doctrinal courses would require professors to rethink their coverage, spend significant time preparing new course components, and completely redesign their class plans."[29]

"While identifying course units seems quite straightforward, this was a surprisingly challenging aspect of the TBL preparation for me. When I converted my instruction to TBL, I had been teaching this course for many years and never characterized the material in terms of 'units.' However, TBL is a backward-design teaching methodology. Professors start with what they absolutely want students to know at the end of the semester and then design backward with those learning objectives in mind."[30]

Then, professors must craft reading/viewing assignments to prepare the students for the class engagement, they must draft the readiness assurance tests, and then design the launch of the individual group classes – formidable tasks to be sure.

The Team-Based Learning Collaborative, an international teachers group promoting TBL, define it as a "form of collaborative learning designed around units of instruction that are taught in a three-step cycle of student preparation, in-class readiness assurance testing, and application-focused exercises."[31]

Some refer to some forms of TBL as "Flipping the Classroom."[32] That title becomes clear when one considers the process. Unlike the traditional class room technique, with TBL and "flipping," the students gain <u>first exposure</u> to new material outside of class, via readings, lecture videos, etc., yielding basic levels of cognitive work, that must be taken seriously because of the readiness assessment tests required prior to the first in-class engagement. This is more productive than the traditional model of teaching in which the students' initial, serious exposure to materials occurs in the class lecture, followed by the students assimilating knowledge through subsequent homework. In Team Based Learning, the process is flipped

---

and the Institute for Law Teaching and Learning website at www.lawteaching. org.

29  Balsam, *supra* note 14, at 262–63.

30  Weresh, *supra* note 13, at 313.

31  Balsam, *supra* at 263.

32  A form of TBL has also been titled "Flipping the Classroom," as described in sources as diverse as The New York Times (Fitzpatrick, 2012), The Chronicle of Higher Education (Berrett, 2012), and Science (Mazur, 2009).

with a structure that demands that students prepare before the first class on the subject. Then the actual class time may be used for more dynamic, interactive higher levels of cognitive work, assimilating the first knowledge with problem-solving, discussion, debates (according to Bloom's Taxonomy, in class application, analysis, synthesis, and evaluation.).

Professor Weresh elaborates: "Faculty members are employing "flipped" techniques that require students to engage more deeply in instructional material outside the classroom, enabling professors to apply concepts and principles more actively in class. Team-Based Learning (TBL) is a form of flipped instruction that has been widely used in other disciplines, and it is now making its way into in legal education."[33]

Again, details are important: Professor Weresh advises that the teams should be "strategically formed, diverse, and permanent (to avoid social loafers). Diversity within groups is essential to avoid barriers to group cohesiveness, including the formation of coalitions within groups."[34] The student groups should be organized in teams of five to seven students and should work together throughout the course. Student groups are formed with a design to accomplish the learning goals – these should not simply be groups of friends, but rather students can be chosen randomly or using students' own assessment of the assets they bring to the class, and then put in balanced groups by the professor. Some professors may wish to use other factors as well, as transcripts or other distinguishing factors. The principal idea is to create balanced groups and avoid recreating usually less productive social cliques.

Likewise, it is fundamental to insure that the students adequately prepare their reading or viewing prior to class. According to the TBL models, this process is not left to the students' discretion, but rather is enforced by what many term a "Readiness Assurance Process," involving two layers of testing.[35] At the beginning of the first class on the subject, each student participates in a Readiness Assurance Process that comprises an *Individual* Readiness Assurance Test, often a multiple-choice quiz to make sure that the students have read the assigned materials before the first class on the unit and assimilated that material. They must understand the foundational substance before they can participate in the discussion dynamic in the groups. "Class begins with a closed-book multiple-choice test that uses

---

33  Weresh, *supra* note 13, at 303, 303–04.
34  Weresh, *supra* note 13, at 310.
35  See *e.g.*, Sparrow, *supra* note 16, at 158–159.

questions that fall on the lower level of Bloom's taxonomy – understanding and remembering."[36]

Then in that first class, the *individual* tests are followed by each team's *Group* Readiness Assurance Test. In taking the test the second time as a team, students debate and agree on their team's answer, discussing the principles they studied and closely reviewing the material on the test. During that same class, students receive immediate feedback about how well they mastered core concepts, with the professor providing a brief follow-up lecture to correct any misunderstandings.[37]

There can even be an interactive element in the first class that allows the students to appeal their test results, which necessarily requires the students to review closely the subject material, challenge their understanding of it (autodidactic) and then defend their appeal orally in front of peers, explaining why their answers are more correct than other options.

Emphasis on pre-class preparation is designed into this testing system because the students' test scores should count toward the students' final grades in the course.

Next, "the core of TBL is the application phase – it's what makes the TBL classroom look and sound so different from a typical doctrinal classroom."[38] Thus, the students have been pre-prepared for in class application activities that require thinking, making choices about the problem/issue. The students work in teams applying the basic concepts and rules, with the professor "leaning in" on group discussion, offering key clarifying questions.

The application exercise requires four components to be effective: "(1) assignments should always be designed around a problem that is significant to students, (2) all of the students in the class should be working on the same problem, (3) students should be required to make a specific choice, and (4) groups should simultaneously report their choices."[39]

This is followed by peer evaluation, another serious thought-provoking process in which the students must judge and defend their judgments about the quality, practicality, usefulness of their peers' reasoning and conclusions.

For the next class meeting, the students are given more readings to help them assimilate the material and their team's positions. The students work

---

36  Balsam, *supra* note 14, at 265–66.
37  Sparrow, *supra* note 16, at 158–59.
38  Balsam, *supra* note 14, at 266.
39  Larry K. Michaelsen & Michael Sweet, *The Essential Elements of Team-Based Learning*, 116 New Directions For Teaching and Learning 10, 20 (2008).

on the next problem for as many class meetings as it takes, and they advance through the course topics. What a dynamic, autodidactic and socially-reinforced construct!

As I reflect on this model, I see so many possibilities. Examples of project "issues" for an International Trade course could include: 1st Project: Assess & organize the economies of select countries to benefit from comparative advantage; 2nd: Organize the tariff schedules of select countries to protect and promote their resources and economies; 3rd: Negotiate Trade Agreements with other teams representing different countries, to further promote and protect strategic resources; 4th: Negotiate disputes – use national remedies, then bringing claims to the WTO Dispute Settlement System, where the students would argue in prosecution or defense of claims; 5th: Serve as Dispute Settlement Panels members, judging and writing conclusions for the dispute arbitration – or serving as Members of the WTO Appellate Body, assessing the validity of the panel decisions.

In today's heated trade environment, numerous current issues could provide stimulating learning debates, for example the validity of WTO Members using the Article XXI National Security ("necessary for the protection of its essential security interests") exception to justify unilateral imposition of tariffs to protect domestic industries or to limit exports of medical supplies. There would be no short supply of controversial, stimulating topics to energize the students. Much course design food for thought.

*Conclusion*

As we law professors strive to more effectively teach our students, we are surrounded by innovative ideas and scores of pioneering colleagues who are demonstrating a myriad of ways to follow our ambitions. In so many forms, we see dynamic professors working to force energy into their classrooms and their students' learning processes. From live law clinics, to realtime synchronous international courses, to team-based learning, numerous innovative examples surround and support us in our professional journey.

# Distance Learning and Video-Based Academic Contributions: Steps Towards "A World Made New"?[1]

*Rui Guerra da Fonseca*[*]

## A. Introductory notes

Bringing about the topic of modern teaching methods always implies that we are between two points of tension: a need of change and a resistance to that change. Indeed, 'modern' only has to be called for because a 'traditional' way of things remains, but still a 'need of change' is being felt, like a constant look, and the source of this might not be as immediate or identifiable as one would think.

Teaching methods at faculties are not something constantly under evaluation and reflection. They are actually a product of a combination of tradition, bureaucratic demands and possibilities, physical conditions and limitations of faculties' material resources, regulations on students' performance evaluation and the creativity (or absence of it) of teachers. All these aspects must be taken into account if one sets forth to comprehend the dynamics of teaching methods (and there are, of course, other variables that must be considered).

It's also important to distinguish between different levels or cycles of studies. In fact, the combination of those factors and variables is not the same at the graduation level, masters level, PhD studies level, and so on.

This text does not aim at a whole comprehensive perspective of the modernization of teaching methods debate. It will focus on two different aspects: distance learning and video-based scientific contributions. Distance learning is an alternative to class-based lectures, something that we all came to know quite deeply in the previous months. On the other hand,

---

1 *A World Made New* is the title of a famous book by Mary Ann Glendon, with a very telling subtitle: "Eleanor Roosevelt and the Universal Declaration of Human Rights" (Random House, New York, 2001). Of course the topic of the present text is not something to be passionate about as the most important human rights document of our time, but many changes start slow.

\* Professor of Public Law, University of Lisbon, Faculty of Law.

video-based scientific contributions are an alternative to written texts in journals or even book chapters; or even entire textbooks.

These are two different issues but strongly connected for two main reasons. First, distance learning nowadays tends to use video-based contributions, previously recorded or live, as canvas. Second, video-based scientific contributions tend to substitute traditional ways of disseminating scientific knowledge and research. Thus, the two principal outputs of university professors are changing in a very accelerated way, and this is a very strong combination as a motor for change. It should not me assumed that these new ways are going to take over the traditional ones, at least in close future. But we must settle as a starting point for reasoning that they have come to stay.

After addressing these two topics, the text will briefly focus on the experience of the *ELPIS V-Law Review* ("EVLR"), a new initiative by the ELPIS Network that basically consists of an online video law journal. A daring experience, the EVLR was a very motivating project from the outset, challenging traditional ways and paradigms.

## B. *Distance learning: between 'need' and 'acquired taste'*

Distance learning is not a totally new thing. In Portugal, there is a public university entirely based on distance learning ("Universidade Aberta"), and there was in the past — now rehabilitated during Covid times in a different model — a TV based school ("Telescola") in order to reach children in parts of the country poorly served by public schools. Both these experiences provide interesting points for consideration. They were both normal or regular in their functioning, not exceptional, meaning that they didn't begin due to exceptional circumstances. But they intended to respond to the needs of students who had no schools or universities close-by, or simply couldn't afford or take the chance to move to another city for that purpose. So, in a way, these experiences were actually exceptional in the sense that they provided learning in a feasible way, which was not the preferable one, constituted by class-based teaching and learning. In short, they responded to 'the sovereignty of the felt need', to use M. Oakeshott's expression.

Many things are different when we take class-based learning on one hand and distance learning on the other. Those differences seem to be much more complex and profound than a simple binomial reduction to success/unsuccess or better results/worse results can explain. Teaching and learning are a societal activity that always took place with teachers and students face to face. There always was *epistola* exchanging, and of course books 'turned the table' on this face to face reality, specially since Gutenberg. Nowadays we still have possibilities for university students to complete their graduation only by making final exams, without attending a single class if they don't want to (in a three or four year graduation it is certainly a matter of will not to attend a single class…), studying only with their books and other written (and nowadays not only…) materials. But, again, this has never been the main stream of teaching and learning because of the societal nature of this activity. Even if I'm not qualified to look at these issues in a scientific or professional way (e.g. pedagogical, social, psychological, anthropological), I feel compelled to lay down a couple of observations which settle on two main aspects: first, they consider fundamentally the teaching and learning of legal disciplines in faculties of law; second, they intend not to depart from a judgmental perspective of these two forms of teaching and learning in terms of good or bad.

Distance learning lays on the same basic patterns of class-based teaching and learning: the teacher transmits knowledge and the students absorb it; the teacher motivates students' participation either with questions or requesting their observations, and by creating an environment in which they feel free to interrupt, posing questions or giving their opinion on a certain subject. All this (and variations) happens or can happen both in class-based and distance learning. The adopted model can be more traditional, sitting on the teacher's performance and activity, or innovative, laying on a greater autonomy of students called to a smarter preparation of subjects and classes. But the basics are the same: the transmission of knowledge from a teacher to a class.

The contact *in personae* is of course lost in distance learning (considering that by *in personae* we mean physical presence). This loss is commonly pointed out, and even dramatically, as the most important negative implication, and the societal aspects of teaching and learning along with it as a consequence. But these are two different aspects: a Venn's diagram would certainly identify common areas, but not a juxtaposition of both. Some societal aspects are lost due to the nature of the means used but happens also in other activities. For instance, you loose the incoming and outgoing of students, the professor coming down the hall, the dressing code (partially: from the waist down…), the concept of silence (you can turn off your microphone and sneeze at will at home), moments of humor (but can gain others, e.g. when a child enters the 'class-room' our living rooms or home studies have turned into). With the generalization of online instruments, namely due the Covid-19 situation, these societal losses also take place in other activities like meetings, conferences and seminars. In situations like these, it's commonly accepted that physical presence is desirable, at least in a certain moment if there is sequence. The first or one in a series of meetings in a certain project should be *in personae* but not necessarily all of them. The same goes to a seminar or equivalent. This means that if we preserve a certain portion of physical presence then the loss of societal points drops considerably.

The justification for this has certainly to do with the positioning of the individual *vis a vis* the other elements of the group and the projection of a personal image *vis a vis* those other elements. In a classroom, this has a very specific manifestation: the authority (not the power) of the teacher or professor *vis a vis* the students. Authority means acknowledgment or recognition, and must not be confused with power (means to an end): so, to be clear, the issue here is not the orders or the prohibitions or the liberties that a teacher can give in a classroom (nor, of course, any kind of disciplinary means of power). The authority of the teacher or professor has many facets and subtleties and we cannot analyze them here. But it is well known its importance within the system of teaching and learning, as kind of a cement. A semester, or even an entire year of a certain school subject, is a path that must be followed both individually and as a class and the authority of the teacher provides an important and powerful guidance for students who are in need of precisely that.

Teacher or professor authority and all its implications are among the most common reasons for looking upon distance learning with a certain mistrust, even if it is not said exactly like that. This seems to disturb both teachers and students. Teachers tend to feel that distance learning makes it more difficult to get the pulse of the class and grasp individual needs. Students seem to feel sometimes lost and to experience greater difficulty reaching the teacher. These are different sides to the same problem.

Presently, we are under the boot of Covid-19 which created an extraordinary need for distance learning. All of us had to adapt and change rapidly and our most common views seem not to take into account two fundamental aspects. First, if we intend to discuss the future of distance learning, we should not forget that the present situation will change: class-based learning was not abandoned forever nor did the paradigm change. Second, the resilience of the traditional model will certainly not be so atavistic to the point of outcasting every manifestation of distance learning now that we've experienced that it has positive aspects.

The combination of distance and class-based learning will certainly be the future for so many reasons among which we can find technological development, the growing numbers of students, but also socio-economic differences. This combination might very well come to be a democratic demand offering different types of students opportunities they wouldn't have otherwise (like with the 'Telescola' in Portugal). We should not discard the possibility of the combination between class-based and distance learning reaching, in time, the status of a human rights obligation for states if it proves to be essential regarding the right to education and other connected human rights, namely in a global society that is just waking up for pandemic threats and circumstances alike.

Thus, the relationship between teachers and students must evolve factoring in this and other changes. In the future, and already presently, distance learning can be an exceptional necessity, from time to time, but it also will be a powerful and resourceful alternative on a more regular basis (e.g., for sick students, for teachers who must attend a conference abroad and want to transmit it to their students or simply to give their class from a distance thus avoiding rescheduling, etc.).

Regarding teacher authority in the context of teacher/students relationship, this must be regarded as an opportunity for evolution and reinforcement. It will certainly take some kind of mastering of new technological instruments, but it will even more likely depend, for teachers, on mastering their availability towards their students and creative ways to transmit knowledge. The act of speaking (as in a lecture) happens differently online than in physical presence. We all know this from watching Tv, webinars, online videos, etc.; namely a clearer speech is needed, with less pauses and 'hick-ups' that normally are compensated by gestures and environmental details or simply 'pardoned' in a much different way than in a video (online or not). This requires preparation, training, getting used to new ways, but then again, just as teaching does.

In a way, distance learning comes as a leverage for reforms in the university cosmos and for refreshment in the relationship between students and professors. Let's face it, a lot of the teaching activity already takes place outside the classroom: through blogs, by email, exchanging papers, online clarification of grades and assessment of reports or dissertations, and even online chatting with students (for the bolder professors...). Also, lots of digital tools have already been imported to the classroom, namely presentations ('power-point' style), videos, movies, and even the online participation of fellow professors from foreign universities when it's not possible to bring them to the classroom. So, distance learning is just a step forward.

It's fundamental to maintain personal contact with physical presence, which in my view should correspond to the highest percentage of contact period in a course. But we must be ready to decrease that percentage when needed, even to zero if there is no plausible alternative, be it because of a pandemic or because building or reparation works on the faculty facilities

151

can no longer be delayed. Professors must find ways to motivate themselves for these new ways or their frustration will very rapidly be identified by their students which may harm their relationship beyond repair.

## C. *Video-based academic contributions: at first one finds it strange…*[2]

As with classes, academia tends to be very conservative in what comes to scientific contributions. Traditionally, they are written on paper — books, journal articles, research papers, etc. — or given as oral presentations — at conferences, colloquiums, seminars, masterclasses and alike.

Within the written *forma*, paper has long lost its monopoly, though: e-books, e-journals and digital files (pdf and other document formats) have been gaining ground for the past two decades, mostly, and are now indispensable. In fact, digital formats and platforms allow us to carry around entire libraries, search for certain expressions (which a good index can provide on a paper book but never as flexible), share our texts much faster and easier, and also faster and more practical proof reading! Still, from an author's perspective, most of the times the work behind a paper book or article in a paper journal is pretty much the same than the work behind an e-book or paper in an e-journal. From the publishers' perspective it's a world of difference (materials, production, distribution, selling, storing, etc.). From the readers' perspective, there are the advantages already mentioned; the rest are tastes like the touch of paper that some of us don't dispense with, at least regarding certain publications…

On the other hand, conferences, colloquiums, seminars, masterclasses and alike still take place in physical presence in a much higher percentage *vis a vis* online or distance means than digital formats to paper. This, of course, considering pre-Covid times, for after the pandemic spread everything rapidly changed to an exclusive on-line model: our living rooms and home offices became everybody's conference room, classroom and webinar or symposium auditorium.

---

2  In 1929, Coca Cola asked a Portuguese advertising company ("Hora") to plot a strategy to enter the Portuguese market. Fernando Pessoa, who came to be one of the most worldwide known Portuguese writers, and worked for the company at the time, came up with an astonishing slogan. In Portuguese, it goes "Primeiro estranha-se, depois entranha-se". The effect of the rime is lost when it's translated to English, but literally in a very free translation it means "At first one finds it strange, but after it roots into you", or more idiomatic "strange at first, wonderful at last". It's still pointed out today as one of the greatest slogans in Portuguese advertising.

Video-based academic contributions ("v.b.a.c.") are an alternative to written books, book chapters, journal articles, papers and others alike, wether they are in paper format or digital format. They are an alternative precisely because they are not written nor read; they are recorded and viewed / listened to. Apparently v.b.a.c. are very different from written books and journals. One could say that their differences are similar to the ones between books and movies. But it just isn't so. If we take a minute to observe, we will see they are not necessarily so distinct; and, most importantly, there is no insurmountable gap of academic or scientific quality between written contributions and v.b.a.c.

Take audiobooks and podcasts: they have been gaining ground in the past decade not only because they are practical but because their quality has consistently augmented. I say this with a much wider knowledge of podcasts than audiobooks. But the fact is that the offer of audiobooks in the legal field (non-fiction) is growing and that only happens because there's demand (and in a particularly orthodox environment, we should say).

A v.b.a.c., as with an audiobook, is usually built or recorded on the basis of a written text which is read or used as the basis for the presentation. The authors may read exactly what was previously written or allow themselves a certain degree of distancing from the text. But the final outcome is not a sequence of spoken bullet points, rather it corresponds to a spoken text that should be ready for (re)transcription and reading if needed. In this sense, there is no difference between the substantive contents of a v.b.a.c. and a written text, meaning that the difference of the 'vehicle' will only reflect different contents if the authors so choose, not by its nature.

One aspect that is very characteristic of legal academic texts are citations and footnotes or endnotes that usually embellish written academic contributions, and I've already heard about the difficulty to put them in a v.b.a.c. as an obstacle. In fact, bibliographical citations or other sources' citations are essential in an academic and scientific work; and we can say that in law they play a special role for they demonstrate a *communis opinio*, or a majoritarian (or the opposite) trend in legal thought, or just intend to atribute the originality of an idea or passage to its actual owner, all of these academically indispensable purposes.

Nevertheless, it is possible to do all this in a v.b.a.c.: it only takes imagination, resourcefulness and will. The citations can be inserted in their exact location as in a written text and read out-loud; a written file can go along with the v.b.a.c. with the citations, and each one duly marked during the reading at the correct location (which can be done in various ways). I've seen many suggestions and ideas for this, motivated precisely by academic seriousness and honesty, showing that — again — technological evolution must always go along with the ethics of each field.

The scientific quality and accuracy of v.b.a.c. is of course a major concern, but doesn't need to be bigger than the one with written texts. And peer reviewing is possible in the same terms, surely not by pre-visualizing the v.b.a.c. — which would brake anonymity — but through the revision of the text which constitutes the basis of the v.b.a.c. It's even possible, before publishing, to compare the final version of the v.b.a.c. with the previously reviewed text — but this is already fine-tuning.

At the end of the day, it doesn't seem to exist any justification to refuse v.b.a.c. On the contrary, v.b.a.c. allow new ways of accessing scientific content and of time management: for instance, a student going to the faculty might find it hard to read in a bus or train because it's bumpy or overcrowded, but listening or watching v.b.a.c. can be much easier.

During exceptional times, like Covid-19, v.b.a.c. can also present an alternative for both authors and students, because of the less dependence on publishing houses.

Who knows? In the (near) future maybe we will take a step ahead. Presently, many paper books already come with a digital copy for the purchaser's use only, and even with their audio fellows. Perhaps it will become normal to receive a book or article in all its formats: written (paper and digital), audio and video. It's a brave new world.

### D. *The* ELPIS V-Law Review *("EVLR")*

The *ELPIS V-Law Review* ("EVLR") was an original idea of Professor Vasco Pereira da Silva, President of the ELPIS Network, as a way to maintain the proximity between the partners of the Network in times of Covid-19 and, at the same time, as an initiative to power up the recently created ELPIS Research project. It was immediately tagged as a perfect combination, specially in this exceptional period during which it was not possible to hold the usual meetings this close group is used to and cherishes so much.

The challenge, as it was sent to all Network partners, was for each member to produce a video, from five to ten minutes, regarding the effects of 'corona virus' in the global, european and national legal environments. The success of this initiative was confirmed by the number of participations received and the enthusiasm of the various members which was clearly showed by the length of the videos (they all exceeded the time limit, and so the title of this first issue had to be changed for "*10 to 15 Minutes on: The effect of the "corona virus" in Global, European and National Law*").

Of course this initiative was largely inspired by the academic reality motivated by Covid-19: the total substitution of class-based teaching by distance learning had a chilling effect on publishing houses, all conferences and international meetings canceled, no flying, severe restrictions in crossboarding or even closed boarders, difficulties acquiring books and other publications.

In this sense, EVLR wouldn't most certainly have been born now and the way it did if it was not for Covid-19. I guess we can say that once again ELPIS played its part bringing about the original meaning of its name: the hope for something good to come along.

The first issue of EVLR is somehow experimental. The greatest freedom was left to the authors: some recorded a video with no interruptions and others with interruptions; some used presentations and others didn't. Even the subjects were bound only by the title of this first issue but leaving lots of room for creativity: as an example, Francisco Balaguer Callejón presented *50 Cartoons for ELPIS*, a very unorthodox artistic approach to the topic. But this last example is very telling: such a contribution would hardly have a place in a classic legal journal, while EVLR potentializes it. It was important to leave space for the authors' creativity and adaptation also so it would be possible to test the potential of EVLR. Here is the table of contents, following Professor Vasco Pereira da Silva's "Editorial — The Challenge": *EU Competences and Pandemic Response — An Overview*, by Claas Friedrich Germelmann (Leibniz Universität Hannover); *50 Cartoons for ELPIS*, by Francisco Balaguer Callejón (Universidad de Granada); *The State of Health Emergency in France due to the Covid-19 and the Marginalization of Parliament*, by Sylvia Brunet (University of Rouen Normandie); *The Criminal Law behind the Masks*, by Gerhard Fiolka (Universität Freiburg Rechtswissenschaftliche Fakultät); *Public Procurement Procedures in Times of Pandemic*, by Maria João Estorninho (University of Lisbon Faculty of Law); *Meteoric Change and Uncertainty — Our Dark 2020*, by Patrick R. Hugg (Loyola University College of Law, New Orleans); *Four Short Notes and a Poem on Portuguese Environmental Law in "State of Emergency"*, by Vasco Pereira da Silva (University of Lisbon Faculty of Law); *Restrictions on Fundamental Rights in Germany in times of Corona*, by Arndt Künnnecke (Federal University of Applied Sciences for Public Administration); *"State of emergency" and "situation of calamity": blurring the legal conditions for fundamental rights restrictions*, by Rui Guerra da Fonseca (University of Lisbon Faculty of Law); *EU State Aid Law – Necessity for a EU Regulation de eminentibus*, by Dimitrios Parashu (Leibniz University of Hannover); *Some Thoughts on the Limitation of Freedom of Religion in the Context of the Covid Crisis*, by Miguel Assis Raimundo (University of Lisbon Faculty of Law);

*WHO is the global guardian of public health?*, by Elvin Evrim Dalkılıç (Bilkent University Faculty of Law, Ankara); *The Competence of the Federal Council to Enact Criminal Law Provisions in the Covid19-Ordinance*, by Lukas Götti (Universität Freiburg Rechtswissenschaftliche Fakultät).

In the following numbers, EVLR will evolve. In some aspects it might get closer to classic legal journals, but its added value will probably lay on the other aspects that distance EVLR from the former. As already said, EVLR was forged in an exceptional context of distance between ELPIS members and also distance learning, intending to take advantage of it to move forward with new ways of sharing knowledge in the legal academia. As it intends to shorten the distance between ELPIS members, so it certainly intends to shorten the distance between teachers and students, capturing their attention and meeting their expectations and most common tools for learning. Because they really want to learn, and we must know how to show them that we're passionate for teaching them.

# From the Student's Drama Group of Playing Legal Cases through the Mentorprogramme to Social Responsibility – Recent Tendencies in the Renewal of the Legal Education in the Faculty of Law at Eötvös Loránd University

*Balázs Rigó**

## A. *Introduction – The Evergreen Conflict of Theory and Practice in Teaching*

The relation of the academic and practical Materia and their proportion in the legal curriculum are the subject of eternal disputes. Besides and as a consequence of the reorganization of the University of Nagyszombat[1] (Trnava, Tyrnau) and the upgrading it into a royal institute, Maria Theresa aimed to reform the legal education too in an order of 1769 issued by the Hungarian Chancellery.[2] In the curriculum of two years of the legal studies of that time[3] following the compulsory and primary two years of philosophy studies[4], the teaching of the so called "domestic [Hungarian] law" was regulated so that the first year was dedicated to academic subjects, while the second was to legal practice, i.e. judicature. The lecturer was to be the same person in both years. By the end of the course of domestic law, i.e. at the end of the second year, criminal law was to be taught. Moreover,

---

* Balázs Rigó (PhD), Senior Lecturer at the ELTE Eötvös Loránd Universtiy Faculty of Law, Department of Roman Law and Comparative Legal History. ORCID: 0000-0003-0112-9546. E-mail: rigo.balazs@ajk.elte.hu
1 The ELTE Eötvös Loránd University was established in 1635 by Archbishop Péter Pázmány, and originally it was called the University of Nagyszombat. It was renamed into Eötvös Loránd University only in 1950.
2 Pauler, Tivadar, *A Budapesti Magyar Kir. Tudomány-Egyetem története.* [=The History of the Hungarian Royal University of Budapest] Budapest, Egyetemi Nyomda [=reprint. Históriaantik Könyvkiadó 2002] 1880. 70–72. pp.
3 After the two years compulsory curriculum of philosophy, the legal curriculum was enlarged into three years only by the royal decree of 1775 concerning the university. Pauler, op. cit. 73. p.
4 Ratio Educationis. Az 1777-i és az 1806-i kiadás Magyar nyelvű fordítása. [=Ratio Educationis. The Hungarian translation of the edition of 1777 and 1806. (trans. ed. and noted by Mészáros, István)] Budapest, Akadémiai Kiadó, 1981. 166. § [pp. 129–130.].

the task of the teachers were that "in the afternoon hours of that year, courts shall be organized from the students so that they would get to know the legal procedure in practice"[5] The duality of theory and practice was modified due to the consequences of the Ratio Educationis issued in 1777, at the same time when the University was placed to Buda. The royal decree placed the education and research onto more scientific grounds.[6] Due to the Ratio Educationis, the usefulness and uselessness of the legal Materia both for the law students and the public good came to the front. For example, the professors were definitely obliged to refrain from *l'art pour l'art* dogmatic arguing.[7]

The more than a decade long statement of prof. Lajos Rácz, former chair of the Department of Universal Legal History, that the practical legal teaching was pushed into the background, can be regarded as an ever green statement according to the criticism of the law students. We share his views that "the legal practice to be achieved under the university years is maintained fragmentarily in the curriculum at most by the moot courts."[8] However, both in the jurisprudence and in the legal practice, the rhetoric skill is inevitable, it is enough if we consider the lectures of the professors, or the speeches of lawyers in trials. The former was helped by the practice that theology and jurisprudence was even already taught parallel in several universities in the Middle Ages. While the latter is necessary by the continuous presence before the court.

---

5  Pauler, op. cit. 72. p.
6  Pauler, op. cit. 143, and the Ratio Educationis 198.§ [p.156.].
7  Ratio Educationis 187.§ [p. 148.].
8  Rácz, Lajos, *Beköszöntő.* [=Introductory Greetings] In: Fáy, Gergely (ed.), *PK – Az Eötvös Loránd Tudományegyetem Állam- és Jogtudományi Kar Perjátszó Körének kiadványa.* [=PK – A Publication of the Student's Drama Group of Playing Legal Cases of the ELTE Eötvös Loránd University Faculty of Law] Budapest, ELTE ÁJK, 2009. [06 April] [Further: PK] 3. p. We must remark that in the last decade, there was a significant leap in both the numbers of the domestic and foreign moot courts and in the outstanding achievements on them in the Faculty. Among others, it is enough to mention the great wins of the Jessup team in international public law in Washington by Gábor Kajtár and Kata Sulyok, and the great achievements of the team in the International Commercial Mediation competition in Paris by Éva Inzelt and the team in the Media Law Moot Court Oxford by Gergely Gosztonyi as coaches. These great successes, however, do not entail the mass practice of moot courts and procedure in legal education.

## B. The Student's Drama Group of Playing Legal Cases

Partly, these century old dilemmas culminated in the question that Károly Kisteleki, senior lecturer of the above mentioned and former Department of Universal Legal History, present day Department of Roman Law and Comparative Legal History after a fusion in 2011[9], asked from himself. "How can a teacher transfer the Materia so that he/she would TRULY [highlighted in the original source by Kisteleki] attract the students' interest?[10] According to Kisteleki, this task is continuous and it means the constant renewal of the fight of the teacher mostly against him/herself. This is also the reason why by breaking the indifference[11] of the students, Kisteleki is eager to establish a true, living and interactive connection between himself and the student until the very day.[12] The first step in the history of the Student's Drama Group of Playing Legal Cases, which is i.e. a circle of students performing legal trials [further: the Circle] originated in these circumstances too. In the so called course, "Fascisct Governance of States in Europe"[13] in the spring semester in 2004/2005, according to the interactive schedule of the course, Kisteleki advised the students to present the Nuremberg Trial, which was a part of the course, as a play if they are interested to do that. Seven members of the class participated, and they presented a very creative documentary play using multimedia facilities like films, photos, portraits, interviews as well. "It was such a great success, that I would quite felt sorry for having that as a unique occasion and that's it,

---

9  For the history of the Department after the Second World War until the above mentioned fusion, see Rigó, Balázs, *Az ELTE ÁJK Egyetemes Állam- és jogtörténeti Tanszék története a második világháborútól napjainkig* [=The History of the Department of Universal Legal History from the Second World War until Present Days] In: Boóc, Ádám – Sándor, István (ed.), *Studia in honorem Gábor Hamza: Ünnepi tanulmányok Hamza Gábor 70. születésnapja tiszteletére,* [=Festschrift for Professor Gábor Hamza's 70th Birthday] Budapest, Közjegyzői Akadémia Kiadó, 2019. pp. 225–230.

10  Kisteleki, Károly, *Szakmai játékosság vagy játékos szakmaiság?* [=Professional Gamification or Gamified Professionalism?] In: PK (op. cit.) 4. p.

11  Gedeon, Valéria, *Tudományos Diákkör másképpen – Az Egyetemes Állam- és Jogtörténeti Tanszék Perjátszó Köre.* [=An Alternative Scientific Student Legal Circle – The Student Circle of Playing Legal Cases in the Department of Universal Legal History] In: PK. (op. cit.) 8–9. pp.

12  Kisteleki, PK. (op. cit.) 4. p.

13  For the materia see further: Kisteleki, Károly, *A fasizmus államkormányzati megoldásai* [=The Solutions of State Governance in Fascism] In: Rácz, Lajos (ed.), *Egyetemes állam- és jogtörténet: Polgári kor.* [=Universal Legal History: Modern age] Budapest, hvgorac, 2002. pp. 287–307.

therefore in the last lesson meanwhile registering the grades, I had the spontaneous idea to establish a circle for playing various famous historic plays in a somehow institutionalised form if they approved of the idea"[14] – as Kisteleki recalled the past events in the formation of the Cirlce. In the next year, in the autumn of 2005, the initial seven members of the course, being supplemented by two further students established the Student Circle of Playing Legal Cases, which still operates until the present day, i.e. for 15 years ceaselessly.[15] Until nowadays, for more or less periods, there were around 100 students members of the Circle. Certainly, most of them have already graduated and pursue their profession as legal practitioners, but this does not deterrent them that they shall step into a play for shorter roles time to time.

The topics of the performances are based on the decision of the members, while the composition of the actual script is always preceded by research meeting scholar claims. This research does not mean only the analysis and the research for literature. In several cases, like the Case of Eichmann,[16] the Bibó-Trial or the working up of the Mailáth-murder[17], the research in archives, thus for and with primary sources, and/or personal consultations with the scholar expert of the certain topic, ex. about Erzsébet Báthory's-Trial[18] preceded the birth of the script which is practiced at first by reading rehearsals, then by scenes and finally by dress rehearsals. The

---

14  Kisteleki, PK. (op. cit.) 4. p.
15  The original members of the course such as Andrea Faragó, Márta Ferenczi, Fanny Hidvégi, Csaba Millen, Zsuzsa Nyitray, Tamás Szigeti and Viktor Vajda were completed by Balázs Laczó and Balázs Rigó.
16  Thus Viktor Vajda, besides analysing Gideon Hausner's Justice in Jerusalem monography, used original legal documents of the case, selected publications and studies. So he made a deep archive research in the Holocaust Memorial Centre of Budapest as well.
17  János Szolnoki, who wrote even two plays, composed both of them by primary, archive resources. These resources helped him to have novelty both about the personality and family relationships of György Mailáth, national court judge in the 19th century, and István Bibó, scholar in political sciences and former minister in 1956, even for the scholars and present day academic research. At the same time, that Szolnoki was researching and writing a trial on a specific legal case, he was searching for the human being behind the trial and the law. In the Bibó-case, even the personal advices of the son of the protagonist, István Bibó, the younger made credulity and authenticity greater. We must remark that Szolnoki joined the Circle as a senior judge having more than three decades of practice in criminal cases voluntarily because he saw some plays and was attracted to participate.
18  By consulting Gábor Várkonyi on his latest, therefore newest and unpublished results of his research, Dorottya Sáray could work those achievements into the Case

composition of a play always comes from the interest of the certain author, in other words, a case will be a play if there is someone who is interested to work on that. From all these it follows, that the work of the author is not just the composition of a story or dramatize the legal literature, but composition means a scholar research especially in the first phase of the writing. Certainly, the members of the Circle always make criticism on the script depending on their own personal interest and erudition in the given topic. This criticism is supplemented by Kisteleki's professional supervision. Therefore, the script and the in its final form undergoes through several checks before it appears in front of the critical eyes of the public audience of the university.

The topics of these trial-plays is extraordinarily various which comes from the broad horizon of universal or comparative legal history. The first play of the Circle about the conviction of Jeanne d'Arc was the first not just in absolute sense, but regarding the historic time frame, the Middle Ages, it was the earliest too. From the early modern age, evidently there have been more plays: the cases of Father George (Martinuzzi Fráter György, bishop from the 16th century in Hungary), Elisabeth Báthory (Báthory Erzsébet, countess in Transylvania and Upper Hungary in the 16th century), Mary Stuart, Oliver Cromwell, the Salem Witch trial, Jean Calas, Marie Antoinette, Danton were shown. Since Cromwell died on the height of his power in a natural way, his trial was a fictitious trial. This play was an experiment of methodology to examine, interpret and evaluate Cromwell's person and governance in several ways. From the modern age the following cases were treated, Tom Robinson's case on the bases of Harper Lee's To Kill a Mockingbird, the trial of Captain Dreyfuss and the case of Luigi Lucheni, the assassin of Sissi. While from the present the plays are about the trials of Anna Anderson (she pretended to be Anastasia Romanov), Al Capone, Eichmann, the rebels of 1956 in Hungary (István Angyal, Ilona Tóth and the anonym university students), and still connected to 1956 but István Bibó's case was a separate play, and finally from the US case-history Charles Menson's, Alan Passaro's (the murderer of Meredith Hunter) and last but not least O.J. Simpson's case were composed in a play. Obviously, the cases followed one another not in this chronological order and several of them were put on stage more than once. It is apparent

---

of Erzsébet Báthory while she was writing the play. For the new results of Erzsébet Báthory see: Várkonyi, Gábor, *Báthory Erzsébet: Bűnös vagy áldozat?* [=Báthory Erzsébet: Guilty or Victim?] Budapest, Kossuth Kiadó, 2016. pp. 47, and Lengyel, Tünde – Várkonyi, Gábor, *Báthory Erzsébet: Egy asszony élete* [=Báthory Erzsébet: Life of a Woman] Budapest, General Press, 2010. pp. 397.

that the topics are not only in time and space, but in legal field of a broaden horizon. Since, while the Circle treats English, American, French and partly Italian and German cases besides the Hungarian ones, the overwhelming dominance of the criminal cases, especially of murder, are supplemented by the topics of tax law, law of persons, crimes against humanity, or from the legal theory the topics of the right to revolt against power, the legality of the power of the monarch or the right to rule in general etc. have to be mentioned as legally relevant issues in the plays. The professionalism of the legal history part of the plays are shown by the fact that the Circle participated in two competitions of the National Scientific Student Circles in 2009 and 2011.

The Circle did not just rapidly grow out of the initial room in the loft but since 2006 the Aula Magna, i.e. the Ceremonial Hall[19] is continuously full, moreover, even there occurs a hiatus in seats therefore sometimes preliminary registration is needed. This registration is necessary especially in case of new plays that were not already put on stage. The year 2006 is also a milestone in the history of the Circle in the aspect that the plays went towards the theatrical plays in their outfit and dramatic formulation from the earlier documentary treatment. This development is proved not just by the active presence and advises of Bence Harsányi, a professional actor of the Momentán theatre company[20] and the Árpád Jutocsa Hegyi,[21] a theatre director's participation in the work of the Circle, but by the fact that the Circle has been and is being invited frequently to participate in external cultural events, festivals to elevate the level of the event. Thus, the Circle appeared several times in the programme of the Long Night of Museums in the Regional Court of Budapest, and in the National Office for the Judiciary, furthermore, it played in cultural clubs and houses as Kossuth Klub and Bálint House besides appearing at the Pázmány Péter Catholic University. Moreover, outside the capital, the Circle appeared in the Royal Castle in Gödöllő, in Hévíz in a school opening ceremony and finally in Veszprém in the cultural festival called Pannon Unifest where a professional jury awarded the first prize to the Circle. In addition to this list, the Cir-

---

19 The Aula Magna can host around two hundred people, see https://www.ajk.elte.h u/content/aula-magna.g.3 [The date of the last download of all the webpages in this paper, is January 10, 2021.]
20 For the company see: https://momentantarsulat.hu/ for the actor see further: https://momentantarsulat.hu/szinesz/harsanyi-bence
21 For his professional biography see further https://theater.hu/hu/portre/hegyi-arpa d-jutocsa--1731.html and https://hu.wikipedia.org/wiki/Hegyi_%C3%81rp%C3% A1d_Jutocsa

cle appeared in Romania in Nagyvárad (Oradea, Großwardein) and in Kolozsvár (Cluj Napoca, Klausenburg) at the Sapientia University too.

The professionalism of the Circle is also shown that it pays special attention to marketing and the division of labour among the members. It owns a blog, a web and a Facebook page.[22] These online accessibilities provide not just an interface to publish the remarkably decorative and well-designed posters of the events, but they are the pages where educational essays, photos are published about the life and story of the protagonists and of course about the historic age of the cases. The plays are well-documented with video recordings and by professional photographers besides the reports in the official journal of the students of the Faculty, the Jurátus.[23] In the history of the Circle, A further step was done when the Circle gained legal personality, i.e. became an officially registered society in 2016. As a consequence, it is not surprising that the Circle is very popular among the students which manifests in the recruitment that is carried out in annual admission procedures.

This popularity among the students including the members of the Circle and their fellows among the audience, is not just due to the coming to the surface of their hidden or suppressed theatrical vein, or not just even thanks to the desire to act on stage. In the progress of putting a case to stage, the students learn skills that are necessary in their work day after day. For example, during the framing of the script the most obvious skills and aims are the ones for doing research, the accurate and eloquent draft and of course the ones needed for the clear and sound composition. During the debates on the script, among the skills and aims we have to mention the respectful articulation of criticism, the elevation of the level in the culture of debates, the attentiveness, adaptation and adjustment to each other, the teamwork and the division of labour. While during the performance, the eloquent and clear speech, again the attention towards each other, the overcome to the stage fright and excitement, the high level concentration and last but not least the improvement of the memory by learning the dialogues by heart. At the same time, the audience learn the statics and dynamics of the procedure and some parts of legal history without books and swotting in a way that meantime they feel great. Thus, this experience-based learning becomes a true and valid knowledge receiving pro-

---

22  Concerning the online appearance in social media for the blog see: http://perjatsz okor.blogspot.com; for the webpage and another blog see: https://perjatszokor.wo rdpress.com; for the FB page see: https://hu-hu.facebook.com/perjatszokor
23  For further information see: https://juratus.elte.hu

cess also for the active protagonists of the play and for the passive specta-
tors. Furthermore, the reflexions after the play, the discussion about and
the internal debate over the play either among the members or among the
audience may insist the persons on thinking over the legal and historic
dilemmas of the case as well. On the whole, the persons in connection
with and by the Circle take part in a travel in time in the legal world that
they acquire knowledge and skills that they can make immediately use of
in the present.

## C. The Mentorprogramme

From the fifteen-year history of the Circle, it is apparent that certain factors that create communities during the typical five-six years of a student's
university life can evolve into true integrative organizations exceeding the
certain student's university years. In case of the Circle, these factors are the
affection and commitment towards the trial-plays or legal-theatre that established from below an organization whose integrative power is unques-
tionable just because of its half-decade existence.

However, in the age of mass education, the integration of the students
cannot be covered by scientific organizations and workshops, student circles, or even by several parties having some hundred students. Moreover,
the freshmen students feel somehow lost at the university environment,
many of them both in physical and mental sense undergo a change in their
lifestyle, besides the fact that the level of education and the commitment
towards the Materia are far higher compared to that of secondary grammar
schools. This educational and culture shock and the necessity for a deeper
integration were recognised by some young teachers who, as invited lecturers of the Freshmen's Camp in 2013, summarizing their experiences and
being supplemented by other young ones, established a voluntary union
between young teachers under the name Below 40 in the autumn of 2013.
In the beginning, this collaboration was nothing else than a loose group of
teachers who, besides the common thinking on current issues concerning
university and higher education, took up ad hoc cases from the public life
of the university or offered the freshmen students the possibility to take advantage of their advices about university life, learning methods etc. This
guidance manifested next year, in 2014 in the voluntary settle down in the
Freshmen's Camp organized by the Student Council and throughout the
academic year in their being available at the students' disposal. Next year,
in the autumn of 2015, as a consequence of the regrettable cases of the pre-

vious years that came to light, a so called Orientation Days (ON)[24] was held instead of the Freshmen's Camp, which was always organized by the Student Council. This Orientation Days was, has been and is still organized according to the order of the Dean by the Mentorprogramme, more precisely, by its Council for Coordination. The Mentorprogramme, or other in other words the Mentornetwork[25] are made up of the members of the former Below 40, and further young teachers, PhD students voluntarily as an organization formed from below.[26]

The Mentorprogramme, however, has not remained on the level of a loose connection between the teachers. According to order 2/2015. (XI. 18.) of the Dean,[27] it became an organization under the direction of the Dean and led by the co-presidents of the mentors. The organization is autonomous to set up the frames of its activity according to the directives of the Dean and the Faculty Council.[28] The aim of the Mentorprogramme is to perform professional activity that helps and orientates the first year students to become a university fellow and promotes talent-scouting (mentoring).[29] These tasks, i.e. the mentoring activity of the students divided into study circles (study groups) are carried out by the members of the mentor network who are formally assigned by the Dean.[30] Point 3 of the order of the Dean is of special significance, because it states that the mentor network takes part in the organization of the Orientation Days.[31] Yet, the real organization is executed by the organizing committee (Council for Coordination), which is both a part of the Mentorprogramme and a parallel operating body of five members assigned by the Dean annually.[32]

---

24  For the Orientation Days see: https://www.ajk.elte.hu/content/ajk-orientacios-nap ok-2019-ajk-on.e.1055

25  For the official and general webpage of the Mentorprogramme see: https://www.a jk.elte.hu/mentorprogram and https://hu-hu.facebook.com/mentorprogramelteaj k/. For an interview about the establishment of the Mentorprogramme with former co-presidents, Sára Hungler and Péter Báldy see: https://jogaszvilag.hu/a-jovo-jogasza/vigyazo-szemek/

26  For the members' introduction see further: https://www.ajk.elte.hu/mentorprogra m/oktatomentorok

27  For the text of the order and other order on the Mentorprogramme see further: https://www.ajk.elte.hu/mentorprogram/szabalyzatok

28  2/2015. (XI. 18.) order of the Dean point 4.

29  Ibid. point 1.

30  Ibid. point 2.

31  Ibid. point 3.

32  Ibid. points 24–25 and 28. The organization is supported in the administrative tasks, especially in the correspondence of the freshmen students by the Office of

Since the newly enrolled students' first meeting either with the university, or their fellow students or even their profession occurs on the Orientation Days, the successful arrangement of the event is of overriding importance both in the aspect of the integration to the university and orientation in the legal profession. This objective is followed in the schedule of the Orientation Days, in which a series of programmes concerning the teambuilding and the legal profession help the freshmen students to commence the first semester in a friendly environment surrounded by fellow mates and with a bunch of practical information supporting the legal Materia. The event for all the enrolled regular students of the Faculty, i.e. the students of law, political science and criminology serve as a basis for integration both in their profession and in their community, which can be widened in the university years. Thus, the Orientation Days is not just an event organized for law students, but as a consequence of its content and schedule, the students of political science and criminology can have the same experience as the law students.

The topic of the first day of the Orientation Days is the Faculty as a community. To achieve this objective, the schedule is figured out so that the students could get to know each other as much as it is possible in this short period and so that they could form an open, honest and uniting community where each opinion is valuable and contributes to the common decisions. This goal is endeavoured with educationally precisely planned tasks and games for teambuilding by the mentor teachers and mentor students assigned to the groups of the freshmen students. On the first day, the fellow students, or due to the compulsory study circles in a more accurate way, the groupmates receive exercises to get to know themselves. These tasks of self-knowledge provide opportunity for each of the students both to reconsider and to express their expectations, concerns and fears of the university life that are afterwards discussed openly in small circles among the students. By this means, the students can find answers to fundamental questions like what they can expect from the university and what not. At the same time, they get practical information like system of the academic titles, the address of a teacher in a formal letter or even they get acquainted with the building itself. All the programmes of the first day is carried out by teacher and student mentors who receive preliminary trainings before the Orientation Days, therefore they act as professional trainers in the first day.

---

Administration, personally by Gábor Győri, and in the issues concerning the budget by the Institute of Postgraduate Legal Studies, personally Péter Báldy.

The theme of the second day is the Faculty as a source of knowledge. The whole schedule of the day is basically divided into two major parts. In the first part, the students hear a short lecture with an aim to inspire them, or in other words, they receive a take away lecture for their university years about what is it like to be a university fellow student, what challenges they must face and last but not least what the profession of law, criminology and political science means in general. After this first lecture, simultaneously, there follow several dedicatedly thought provoking panel discussions led by the mentor teachers where the experts of each topic quasi as keynote speakers allow the student to have a hint in certain topics that will have an effect of the students' profession. For each panel there enrols only one student, thus there will be participants from each of the groups who returning to their original group will summarize his/her own panel discussion to their groupmates. These professional topics, like multiculturalism, law and religion, law and media, globalization, legal activism, crime and media, politics and crime etc. show the diversity of the social effects of the activity that both lawyers, criminologists and the experts of political science perform. In the second part of the day, again in the original groups, the invited lawyers, criminologist and experts of political science or even politicians talk each other and with the students about the beauty and the drawbacks of their own career and job. Since this discussion contrary to the first panel of experts and the serious topics aims to show individual career pathways, the students get a more personal insight to the work and life of the branches of legal profession. The invited persons belong to different types of the legal professions, like to the traditional triad of the legal profession, i.e. the lawyer-prosecutor-judge, or to a more recent one, i.e. governmental-private or non-governmental (civil). Thus the students by groups can have the opportunity to get some knowledge and first-hand experience on the work of jurists. Certainly, in this panel of career discussions, the role of the anecdotes or even some paternal care towards the freshmen students occur easily while in the discussion of the experts, this happens rarely.

The closing third day is about the opportunities. This day partly combines the experiences of the communities of students with the professionalism and career-orientated aspects of the second day. During the day, both the organizations of the whole university and those of the faculty and the students introduce themselves. Thus, the freshmen students can meet and get familiar among many others with the University and Faculty Libraries, the Erasmus Office, the Centre of Career etc. The backbone of the participants is made up of the student organizations, student scientific circles, colleges for advanced studies, student associations and clubs. The objective of these organizations on the very first day of their meeting with the students is the promotion, the PR activity and obviously, the recruitment. Therefore the participating organizations wait and attract the students among others with interactive games, tiny gifts of entertainments, self-made videos and quizzes. During the day, it is possible to participate in accompanying programmes such as simulation of a criminal trial, visiting a mobile cell brought to the court of the faculty, listening to a round table debate on several topics, or even having discussions with teachers of the faculty, who are living books that can be borrowed by the students for the time of the discussions in this so called living library. At the end of the day, as a closing activity of this three days, the mentor teachers and mentor students discuss the experiences of the days with the purpose of reflection.

After the Orientation Days, the mentor teachers and students hold practical classes during the whole academic year that are of great benefit during their whole university studies, but are especially important in the first year, when the freshmen are facing significant challenges and expectations compared to their secondary grammar studies. These classes include methods of learning and writing, time-management, moreover, by the shadow of the fore coming exam period the students receive advices for their first exam period of their life. The latter event covers in the first place the practical side of the exam period, thus, the aim of this activity is not at all to repeat the content of a subject, but to show the differences between a university exam and a test of the secondary grammar school or even the final exams of the secondary studies. Furthermore, the mentor teachers hold individual, i.e. face to face discussions with the students where they touch the adapting of the students to the new university life, the possible personal problems in this new stage of their personal development. If it is of great necessity, or the teacher has doubts of the students' personal environment and behaviour, it is his/her duty to advise the student to the mental expert or even to psychologist of the faculty.[33]

This mentoring activity occurs during the first year of the students as far as possible by having two mentor teachers and three mentor student in each group. Both the teachers and the students enroll voluntarily to be mentors. The previous ones are appointed by the Dean, while the mentor students are selected by the Mentor programme, i.e. the mentor teachers and the Council of the Students in a multilevel entrance procedure. The mentor teachers are mainly among of the young teachers and PhD students of the Faculty. The Mentor programme is directed by two annually

---

33  Ibid. point 9.

elected co-presidents[34] who represents the Programme before the Dean and the Faculty Council. Regarding its organization, it consists of the Body of the Mentors and a Coordination Council for organizing the Orientation Days, and of an Ethic Council. The Body of the Mentors hold one assembly in each month. While the operative and everyday activity is carried out by the so called Programme Group, which is responsible for organizing social and teambuilding cultural events, the Training Group, which is responsible for the training of the members and finally, the psychological-educational cases are handled by and discussed in the Case-Group, which is involving the psychologist of the Faculty.

## D. *Social Responsibility*

Besides the obvious integrative role and purpose, the success of both the Circle and the Orientation Days, on the one hand, shows that the students are responsive to them. While on the other, the students need that surpassing the introduction of legal problems and the legal profession in the narrow sense, they should meet the broad society and its wide problems preferably in practice too during their studies. Since, as they learn to recognize the law behind the social problems, thus vice versa, they should notice the society behind the law as well. This objective was to be achieved by the course called social responsibility[35] that was launched in the spring semester of 2018 with the dedicated support of the Cabinet of the Faculty, especially the enthusiasm of the vice-dean, Réka Somssich, the Mentorprogramme and the Student Council by Károly Kisteleki, the founder of the Circle, mentioned above.

The aim of the course is the establishment of a kind of service learning so that the type of activities of voluntarism and community service should be known and available to the students. Within the framework of this activity, the students gain professional and social experiences while they are performing beneficial deeds for the community. Furthermore, by this activity, they acknowledge and admit implicitly that they belong to the luckier minority of the society who have the opportunity, time and knowledge

---

34 Until now, the co-president were Valéria Kiss and Károly Kisteleki in the academic year of 2015/16, Sára Hungler and Péter Báldy 2016/17, Anna Rácz and János Fazekas for two years, in 2017/18–2018/19 and the present pair is Anna Rácz and Imre Képessy 2019/2020.

35 For the online appearance in social media see: https://www.facebook.com/elteajkt fk/, https://www.instagram.com/elteajktfk/

to work for others. The students perform the activity offered in the course in a very organized way, in safe environment and by the tutoring of experts so that the aims, expectations and basic values become clear for all the parties. By trying the students on the spot and in harsh situations, the course provides a sort of experience in learning and the development of skills of sensitivity towards social problems. Therefore, the knowledge acquired earlier is completed by the reality of life. At the end of the course, the students treat all these experiences both in writing and orally with the tutorial of the teachers in a structured way in order to have the most self-reflection as possible after the course. The most important values to be transmitted are the openness, the positive thinking, the solution-orientated approach, the acceptance and the toleration.

The course in voluntary in the way that the students take it as a subject from the curriculum on their own, free choice. For meeting the requirements of the course, they get [ECTS] credits, which is the registered award or prize for their service. This frame of the higher education also determines that the rules of the act on traditional voluntary service[36] are not applicable for the students enrolling for the course. The voluntary service is manifested in the activity performed for the community, however, contrary to the secondary grammar school, it is not a compulsory part of the curriculum. Self-evidently, the activity performed during the course is not labour, therefore among others it is not recompensed by any fee, right to pension etc. The course can be taken at most in two semesters.

At the beginning of the course, the students participate in a lecture treating the characteristics of social responsibility and the difference from voluntarism, labour and community service. After getting connected to the chosen organization, they perform the tasks and duties appointed them by the organization itself. This makes up at least eight times one and a half hour, and must be performed at least on two different days, i.e. in one occasion, practically in a long day, the course cannot be fulfilled. After the activity in the organizations, the students are divided into small groups, where they present their own organization and activity for the others. Finally, they make a short composition on the same topic. The organizations being involved in the course vary on a broad spectre. Among others, the student can choose between organizations such as foundations, societies or associations etc. dealing with education, environment or animal protection, the homeless, sick children or children permanently in hospital, the

---

36 Act LXXXVIII of 2005 on Voluntary Service. For the text of the act see: https://net.jogtar.hu/jogszabaly?docid=a0500088.tv

old-aged, the blind or deaf people, the disabled or the mixture of these categories etc. Among the organizations, there can be found small local and multinational, global organizations for example Bátor Tábor Foundation (children camps), Budapest Bike Maffia and Heti Betevő (food donation), inDahouse and Kórházsuli and Magosfa (education), Menhely Foundation and Trappancs Association (animal protection), National Institute for the Blind, the Hungarian Charity Service of the Order of Malta, WWF Hungary, Unicef etc. The course started with 13 organizations, while in the spring semester of the academic year 2019/2020, the students could choose between 26. The number of the students depends on the size and the profile of the organization and vary generally between 3 and 5 persons, but the maximum number in an organization is 20 persons. The experience is that the students enrol for the 50–60 % of the available positions. In the very first semester of the course, in the spring of 2017/2018 they took 95 from the possible 160 positions, while in the above mentioned spring semester of 2019/2020, i.e. in the last one, they had 133 from the possible 236. The dropout is slightly small, it differs between 5 and 10 %. The number of the participants show that though there is space for development, the more than two dozen of the organizations and the permanent number of c. hundred students deserve high respect on their own.

As a conclusion, we can ascertain that in the Faculty of Law at ELTE several pioneer initiations made its way in the last one and a half decade that could succeed both in the professionalism of legal education and deepen the integration of the students. At the same time, these new approaches do not force the education to choose between the students' need for more practice and the academic level of teaching or when it comes to have a definite side between the artificial separation of human and law. Since, one cannot exist without the other. The jurists and the law exist among the people in society, and day by day they face social and human problems which can be solved only by knowing the social environment. As the success of the above mentioned programmes show us, this problem solving skill can only blossom out from democratic communities consisting socially sensitive and freely acting individuals who respect the private autonomy of each other.

# List of Authors (incl. their University Affiliation and Main Function)

Francisco Balaguer Callejón
Prof. Dr. (Professor of Public Law), University of Granada

Claas Friedrich Germelmann
Prof. Dr., LL.M. (Cantab.), Gottfried Wilhelm Leibniz University of Hanover (Chair for Public Law, especially European Law)

Rui Guerra da Fonseca
Prof. Dr. (Professor of Public Law), University of Lisbon, Faculty of Law

Patrick R. Hugg
Prof. Dr. (Professor of Law Emeritus), Loyola University College of Law, New Orleans, Louisiana (USA)

Kire Jovanov
LL.M. alumnus, Gottfried Wilhelm Leibniz University of Hanover

Arndt Künnecke
Prof. Dr. Dr. (Professor of Public Law), Federal University of Applied Sciences for Public Administration Brühl / Germany

Kersi Kurti
LL.M. student, Gottfried Wilhelm Leibniz University of Hanover

Maria Meng-Papantoni
Prof. Dr. (Associate Professor of European Business Law), Panteion University, Athens (Greece)

Bernd H. Oppermann
Prof. Dr., Dr. h.c. (Rouen), Prof. h.c. (UMCS), LL.M. (UCLA), Gottfried Wilhelm Leibniz University of Hanover (Chair for German, European and International Civil and Commercial Law)

Dimitrios Parashu
Dr. iur., MLE, Dikigoros (Greek Lawyer), Habilitand and Research Associate at the Faculty of Law, Gottfried Wilhelm Leibniz University of Hanover

Vasco Pereira da Silva
Prof. Dr., Dr. h.c. (Hannover), Professor of the Law Faculty of the University of Lisbon (Professor Catedrático da Faculdade de Direito da Universidade de Lisboa)

Balázs Rigó
Dr., Senior Lecturer at the ELTE Eötvös Loránd University of Budapest, Faculty of Law, Department of Roman Law and Comparative Legal History

Andreas Schwartze
Prof. Dr. (Professor of Civil Law), LL.M. (EUI), University of Innsbruck

# Index